My Father, My Son

My Father, My Son

Intimate Relationships

Lee Salk

G. P. Putnam's Sons
New York

Library of Congress Cataloging in Publication Data

Salk, Lee, date.
    My father, my son.

    1. Fathers and sons—United States—
Interviews. I. Title.
HQ756.S18   1982   306.8'7   81-22717
ISBN 0-399-12636-8   AACR2

PRINTED IN THE UNITED STATES OF AMERICA

Acknowledgments

My special thanks to Barbara King for her creative editorial assistance, and to Bill Adler who asked, "Lee, why don't you write a book about fathers and sons?"

I dedicate this book to my father, the late Daniel B. Salk, and to my son Eric Daniel Salk.

My Father, My Son

Introduction

On a blustery winter afternoon in 1944, my father waited with me in Penn Station for the train that would take me away to the army center where I would begin my World War II military service. He looked at me with tears clouding his eyes, hugged me tightly, kissed me on the cheek and told me good-bye in a choked voice. Then, wanting to give me something that was his, he took off his watch and handed it to me.

As I walked toward the train, I looked at my father, who was waving gently and sadly to his seventeen-year-old son, and suddenly I noticed that several people were watching us with bemusement. I sensed then that such an intimate farewell was perhaps unconventional between a father and son. My feeling was emphasized by a family scene occurring to my right. Another father, gravely smiling, gave his son a firm pat on the back and said, "I'm proud of you." I wondered, as I observed this formality between father and son that seemed so odd to me, how they *really* felt about each other. And I thought how different it was—how different it had always been—with my father.

Daniel Salk was a tender, affectionate, compassionate man who laughed easily, who talked freely to strangers, who loved sitting in Central Park feeding the pigeons and squirrels. I think back on his innocent delight as the pigeons would light and eat from his hand. I can vividly recall the feel of his whiskers and the smell of his skin when he would hug me or when he would pick me up and then lift me high into the air—a daily routine when he arrived home from work. And how I loved walking with him, holding on to his index finger and pressing his hand so I could watch his veins swell out. I can recall, too, how much he wanted to make me happy, even though he could scarcely afford even the simplest pleasures. He was something of a Willy Loman character from *Death of a Salesman,* beaten down in business but still believing that success would soon be his. Once when I was six, he took me to an amusement park in Rockaway Beach, where we lived during the Depression. People around us were happily playing games; I could see my father's dismay because he wanted me to have the same enjoyment. Impulsively he pulled a nickel from his pocket, slipped it into a machine, and said, "Enjoy yourself." "It's okay, Pop," I told him, "I'm having fun. You don't have to spend your money." I felt guilty over his sacrificing even a nickel, but he did it with sincere relish.

He was openly proud of all three of his sons. When the announcement was made on April 12, 1955, that his eldest son, Jonas Salk, had developed the first polio vaccine, he was exhilarated, and long afterward he would show newspaper clippings of that historic day to strangers. The stature he acquired from the success of his children made up for whatever struggles he had had in attempting to achieve his *own* success.

The imprint of Daniel Salk's personality is deeply imbedded in my brothers and me. We find it entirely natural to be physically demonstrative with both our female *and* male children, hugging and kissing them just as our father did us.

When my son Eric was born twenty years ago, I wanted desperately to be present in the delivery room, but then this was automatically prohibited in hospitals. One was considered peculiar even to make the request. The best I could do was manage to be present in the labor room, though not without pressuring and cajoling the authorities. Immediately after his birth, before he was bathed, I was given permission to see him. His eyes were wide open and he was very alert. We had direct eye-to-eye contact, and I will never forget the intensity of my emotions at that moment and the strong feeling of bonding it created in me.

Right from birth, I became intricately involved in the rearing of my son. On weekdays, when most fathers were at work, I would spend hours with my toddler at a playground in Central Park. I couldn't help noticing the questioning looks that mothers, nurse-maids and baby-sitters gave me. I knew they must be wondering: Why isn't this man working? Is he unemployed? Where is his wife? Without a doubt, this was not what fathers were expected to do. Only a few years later I was asked to write an article for a leading family magazine about fatherhood. Since the article was to be the lead story, I asked the editor to do what I had never seen done before: put a father on the cover holding a baby. In that article, I presented a strong argument in support of fathers taking a nurturant role in the care of their children, since I believed that males had a deep desire to actively participate in child rearing.

Twenty years ago, a man carrying a baby in a sling or wheeling a carriage down the street was unusual, if not aberrant. Today, much to my satisfaction, fathers are encouraged to take classes with their wives in prepared childbirth and to be present in labor and delivery rooms. Birthing rooms are becoming common in hospitals, allowing families to be together during this momentous occasion.

11

Childbirth is at last being considered a family experience rather than a medical experience. Fathers who have shared in the childbirth experience talk about "*our* labor," "*our* delivery." We see fathers in television commercials selling disposable diapers. We hear not only of fathers sharing equally in the rearing of children but of househusbands, who take care of household duties while mothers work outside the home. (One famous proponent of househusbandry was the late John Lennon, who took care of his son Sean during the day while his wife, Yoko Ono, handled their business affairs.) The question of the father being considered a legitimate parent is no longer even an issue. Fathers fight for custody, and often win. Fathers' rights groups have been created to support their demand for equal access to their children. Newspapers and periodicals are published to provide an exchange of ideas for fathers involved in the nurturance of offspring. In the early stages of my career, when I addressed fathers on how to give love and discipline to their children, I was likely to be told by them, "that's my wife's responsibility." Most fathers were placed in the role of paying bills and doling out punishment. Today, I see fathers playing a significant part in the everyday lives of their children. They are not passively accepting these responsibilities, rather they are actively seeking to become participants.

Unquestionably, there has been a profound change in role behavior in our society. I believe that not many generations ago women derived a sense of gratification and worth from their contributions to the family and to the home—making yarn at the spinning wheel, baking bread, and so forth. With the mass production of prepared food, ready-made clothing and disposable items, these once essential, highly respected activities became unnecessary. Many women could no longer gain a sense of importance or recognition for their direct input into the home. Moreover, couples were inclined to have fewer children, and this in a sense minimized even futher the self-esteem a woman could gain from her traditional role as homemaker and child caretaker. Ultimately, these changes led to a reexamination not only of the woman's role within the family, but of the man's role as well. We were forced to reevaluate ourselves, and we began to recognize that the distinctions that had historically been made between the sexes were no longer functionally useful—either to the genders, or to the existence and survival of the family. As a result of the breakdown of stereotyped family roles, a reshuffling has taken place, with males and females sharing in family responsibilities. As Jonathan Piel, the forty-two-year-old editor of *Scientific American Medicine,* put it, "I think perhaps the whole improvement in relationships between men and women dates back to the emergence of the Beatles in the early sixties, to the whole flower-child renovation of feelings about oneself, of what it is to be a woman or man. Suddenly the accepted patterns of behavior broke down and what emerged was a greater feeling of equality, of sharing experiences. There are some historical factors at work here. The Second World War began to break down the economic stereotypes a bit—women had to go to work doing jobs that had been done primarily by men before they all went away to fight. And then the big increase in the wealth of the general population helped make the change possible—in other words, the traditional roles were supported to a large extent by economic necessity; when the economic necessity began to dissolve, the roles also began to change. Critics would call this a blurring of roles, but I think it's a positive development to the extent that traditional roles had unhealthy emotional patterns built into them. The result was that men and women finally began to see each other as people."

And Marne Obernauer, Jr., the thirty-seven-year-old chief executive officer of the Devon Group, Inc., reflects on the effect of these changes in his own life: "In many ways I have the feeling that what is called women's liberation is basically men's liberation. Men have been liberated from a lot of the stereotypes and hang-ups they had. Certainly one of the things *I've* been liberated from is any

13

inhibition I might have had about being physically or emotionally expressive. Male liberation makes my life so much happier because I'm more involved with my children—society has a way of stereotyping and telling you how much involvement you *should* have. It also makes my wife so much happier because she has a full-time career, so we share fifty-fifty in child rearing. This certainly would have been very difficult in my father's era because of the stereotypes, of the manner in which society would frown upon both men and women altering their roles."

Thus we have reached a stage in our social evolution in which femininity is not synonymous with the delicate, helpless, subservient female, nor is the strong, silent macho man consistent with our revised image of masculinity. Men can be openly expressive and candid about the way they feel. We can even tolerate them crying without viewing it as a sign of weakness. And how many people would think it "unmasculine" for a father to feed, bathe, carry, kiss and care for his child?

In light of this new era of self-evaluation and change in our traditional roles, I believe there is a particular need to closely examine the relationship between fathers and sons. It is a relationship that has been fraught with myths and misunderstandings. Since the early part of the twentieth century, Freudian concepts of behavior have pervaded much of our philosophy and literature. Indeed, Freud's theory of the Oedipus complex—that males have an unconscious incestuous desire for their mothers and are therefore locked into the death throes of competitive battle with their fathers—has provided the basis for analysis of male neuroses. The presumption, from a psychoanalytic point of view, is that the father-son relationship is built around conflict, resentment, jealousy, hostility and destructive impulses. Because the focus of psychology has been on pathological behavior, we have tended to base many of our ideas on the negative aspects of relationships. Ironically, Freud himself recognized the affectional ties that exist between fathers and sons. The widespread interpretation of his

Oedipal theory, however, seems largely to have ignored this. Moreover, the tender, nurturant tendencies inherent in males have often been stifled by the "male mystique." Consider this excerpt from *Peer Report,* a publication sponsored by the NOW Legal Defense and Education Fund:

> Growing up male in our society can be tough. Boys learn that it's not enough just to be themselves—they must somehow *prove* they are full-fledged males.
>
> The cardinal rule for boys is "don't be like a girl." Boys find that certain *human* experiences—nurturing others, being aesthetic, sensual, emotional—are taboo, because society labels them "feminine."
>
> Boys may be taught harshly and impatiently to conform to society's expectations of their sex. While parents may view their "tomboy" daughter with tolerance and affection, nobody wants a "sissy" son.
>
> A boy's deepest emotional ties may be with women. After all, women—mothers, grandmothers, preschool, and elementary teachers—raise the children in this country. The demand that he be nothing like the adults he feels closest to can trigger tremendous conflict inside a boy. Studies show a higher level of anxiety in very "masculine" boys who try to do away with everything "feminine" in themselves.
>
> If he can't be like girls and women, who can a boy safely emulate? Since fathers traditionally aren't home much, most boys can't learn "to be a man" by spending a lot of time with them. They may fill the vacuum with distorted information from peers and older boys and from media images—John Wayne, Superman, the Hulk—that could make anyone feel like a failure.

As the report went on to emphasize, many men want to be closer

15

to their children, but the old assumptions that mother means "mommy" and father means "breadwinner" can set up barriers between fathers and children. Under the traditional rules of the game, men have almost no option of staying home. Often their jobs exact a tremendous toll in hours and energy—leaving them little time for their children. And even more damaging, perhaps, is "the rigidity built into the male mystique, the discomfort many feel in the nurturing role because they've been told it's not manly."

In an effort to explore the affectional ties between fathers and sons, we interviewed men from all parts of the country—from the thriving metropolis to the heartland of Middle America. No attempt was made to represent the population proportionately by providing a sampling broken down into percentages; rather, we preferred the approach of the psychological portrait of an individual relationship over the colder, more clinical one of statistical data. In-depth interviews were conducted in the woodlands of Maine and the flat dusty farmlands of West Texas, in skyscraper suites and in middle-class kitchens. A wide range of ages and occupations as well as socioeconomic and ethnic groups are included: a Mexican-American waiter, a corporation chairman, a famous talk-show host. Often four generations are portrayed—men reflecting on their relationships with their fathers and with their sons, and those sons, in turn, spoke of *their* sons.

Although the focus was on affectional ties, no specific questions were prepared; questions tended to be free form and open ended, following the lead of the interviewee and not the interviewer. Nonetheless, consistent themes emerged, the need for physical contact, for spending time together, for discipline. Although it has become something of a cliché to consider the father-son relationship fraught with conflicts, I found little evidence to support this assumption.

Because the interviews speak so vividly for themselves, they are presented here intact. Dissecting them, analyzing the variables point by point, would, I feel, destroy their essence—the intense human quality, and the emotional impact of the way fathers and sons feel about their relationships.

In many cases, names and other pertinent identifiable information have been disguised for the protection of privacy. Where there is an asterisk (*) it indicates that names and places have been fictionalized.

1

A muscular, blue-eyed bachelor of thirty-five, Hal Burkett*
works in a family retail business in the Northwest. He is an
avid sportsman who lives in a rustic, sparsely furnished house
in the countryside.

I would describe my relationship with my father as semi-stormy from the ages of about eleven through seventeen. That was a growing-up period, and there was a generation gap as far as music, entertainment, and so forth. It was quite pleasant in the early years of my life, although there was a lot of discipline. But then I would say it turned out for the best, because I've seen a lot of my peers who weren't as disciplined who turned out to be utter tramps. They didn't go through the regimen, so to speak.

My father was not a gushing sunflower by any stretch. He was affectionate at—oh, how would you put it?—depending on the situation. A gorilla, an alligator, Ursula Andress, everybody has ways of expressing affection, so you might say he had *his* ways of expressing it; however, it wasn't in the traditional sense. I knew it was there, but at the same time he didn't jump up and down with joy. He was never one to be mushy or emotional. I just knew the affection was there in the same respect that you would know if a person is mad. I sensed it. A person can express various moods without saying too much.

If I had a son, I'd be pretty much like my father. I would teach him the basic rules and values. I would describe a good father as one who instills discipline in the sense of values, behavior, hygiene, everything, at a young age, so that a child will get off to a good start. I hope I've inherited my father's common sense and discipline. I think I have, although I've been involved in various life-styles and cultural exchanges that he hasn't, because he's of another generation. But I imagine he did things in his youth that were considered racy by the prior generation. So some things change but the basic values *don't* change.

What I liked about him when I was growing up was his frankness, the fact that he would answer questions as if it were an adult he was talking to. If something was wrong, I knew. He was never one to add any sugar coating. I don't remember any *specific* warm or tender moments. I remember my entire upbringing. I look at it from an overall point of view. He was my basic foundation of support. He did not spare any resource, whether it was time or money or whatever, if I needed him. We had a traditional family; when he came home from work he spent time with us. At the dinner table there was not just idle chatter, there was intelligent conversation. He was always ready in good times or bad times. In other words, he was *there*.

2

Richard Crim is a thirty-year-old offshore surveyor who has lived, for the past five years, in Baton Rouge, Louisiana. A soft-spoken, rather shy man, he is the father of a three-year-old son, Jason.

The period of my life when I felt closest to my father was the summer after I graduated from high school. The two of us built a summer house for our family up on a lake in North Georgia, and it was the longest stretch we had ever spent together—all day long, four or five days a week. In the evenings after we finished work, we sat around in the woods watching the sun set over the lake. We'd start talking about things, and sometimes we'd talk until it was past dinner and all the restaurants were closed. He had always been pretty closed off emotionally, but that summer I began to feel him opening up.

My father was an engineer, and a veteran of World War II. I think his war experience sort of cauterized a lot of nerve endings: it made him separate from people. He fought in Africa and Japan and the Pacific, but he never talked about the war. I got an idea of his involvement from clippings in my aunt's scrapbook. He was a local hero from Miami, and knowing that about him has been one of the things that has always intimidated me, because he was so *special*. I had the feeling I could never live up to that. He was quite an idol to look up to, so I tried all the time for his approval and it was rarely forthcoming.

There was no real physical affection from him. I would get praises for doing a good job in school, but any physical approval like hugging came from my mother. I don't recall wanting it back then, but I have since found that I like it. When I go to visit him and he holds out his hand to shake mine, I just pass right by and hug him. He feels uncomfortable with that, but *I* don't. I have no qualms about holding or hugging or kissing my own son. I hope to continue it as he grows up although from what I hear, kids naturally pull away from it at a certain age. But I don't feel like *I'll* close it off.

The physical affection from my mother didn't make me closer to her than I was to him. It was just a matter of learning that my parents reacted differently to me, so I expected different things. I knew if I wanted comfort for something, I would go to my mother; if I wanted advice, I would go to my father. If I wanted the straight facts—if I was making a new toy, or something—I would go to him. He'd know how to answer me. But if I was having trouble, like when I started dating girls, I'd go to my mother. My father just couldn't deal with emotions as well as my mother.

The summer we built the house, he became more accessible. We talked about things we'd never talked about before—about girls and about my going out and having a beer or two when it was still against the law for an eighteen-year-old. I was not reacting to him as the father-authority figure; it was more person to person. I guess that was the whole gist of it: it was more on a one-to-one level. We discussed things like college. I was facing a big, vast unknown. I didn't know *what* I wanted to do. I didn't want to go to college, and he was encouraging me to go. In fact, he insisted on it, saying he'd pay and that I should go for at least a year so I wouldn't be afraid of going later on. He said that if I didn't, in a few years it would become too large to tackle.

He was a very goal-oriented person, objective about everything. But he never really pushed me toward anything, saying I had to do this or that. That's one thing I admired about him. He didn't lay down the law about what I should do—although I tended to model myself after him anyway. I admired him. He was my *father*. Some people I knew didn't like their fathers. I did. He wanted me to experience lots of things, but he didn't become too rigid about what I could do. When I was in high school, I used to sing in a rock-and-roll band and he thought that was great. At first I expected him to reject the idea. I brought it up anticipating his disfavor, but he thought it was just great. He said, "Do it. Go out and make a million dollars if you can."

When I lived at home, I always succumbed to my parents' rules and discipline. After I left high school, I began to discover myself and then I rebelled, with drugs, but it was purely against the way they wanted me to live. I think a lot of what rebellion is, is just trying on different suits of clothes. So it was never actually a direct rebellion against *them*. No, I never had that.

Any competitiveness I might have felt toward my father involved trying to make it in his eyes; I *still* feel his eyes on me. I feel that I've let him down because I never finished college, which has always been a disappointment to him. He thinks I had the potential to do much more than I'm doing. I am now feeling a lot of inadequacy around him, because I haven't quite measured up to what he expected of me. I'm not operating like I did earlier in my life by trying to satisfy him, however; I'm doing what I need to do for *myself*. But still, in the back of my mind I feel it: not quite measuring up.

My parents live in Atlanta, and I came down to Baton Rouge about five years ago to work. I had been going to Georgia Tech, and I came here temporarily because of the recession. I ended up staying. I bought my house here, became a father here. I've lived here longer that any place else in my life—five years is a long time for a military-raised person. But my parents are after me to move back to Atlanta. They visited me recently and they tried very hard to convince me to come back. I asked them, "Do you bother Jerry? Do you bother my older brother about this, trying to get him to move from Washington?" And they said, "Well, no, he's got an *important* job." My brother is a designer of piping systems for nuclear power plants. His career meets more with my father's approval, I guess. But that comment that he has an important job, that mine is disposable, that really bothered me. It makes me a little angry, and a little resentful that they look on me like that, comparing me to my brother

I would describe my father as very strict, as an authority figure, as too unemotional. Yet, I would describe a good father as sort of like my father—to be authoritative, to be a role model, but to also be there to guide a child, to help him, to teach him. My father's idea of love was simply not connected to physical emotion. I knew he loved me, though . . . it's a feeling *beyond* knowing, really. I felt very secure in my family; they created a warmth and a bond, and I always knew my father was *there.*

There must be whole sides of my father that I don't know—and there are sides of *me* that I'd like to show *him.* I wish that he was more able to reveal himself. I feel that in a sense I inherited his way of dealing with the world. I feel somewhat unable to give of myself, like I would like to. I wrote a poem to my parents on one of my birthdays. I had been writing a couple of years but never told them about it. We got into a discussion of poetry. I had never before in my life mentioned poetry, but it turns out my father is very well read and likes poetry, but he had never let me know. He was a closet poetry lover but he had decided he never wanted to show anybody, I guess. Yet when it came out in me, and I revealed it to him, he responded.

I think my mother and father accepted the roles of society, but

I've departed from that. I participate very much in raising my son. I feel like it's what I should do, in a way. I don't believe my wife should be in it alone. This may partly be a reaction to my father. He was a man's man, so to speak. My feeling for my son had been growing through the nine months of Joan's pregnancy—I was participating in her pregnancy, helping her, massaging her belly. So gradually an emotion grew in me. It was *amazing* when the baby was born. The euphoria I felt! We delivered him at home. We were lucky enough to find an old doctor who had gone to medical school back when that was the way to do it, so he still delivered babies at home. I had to assist him and Joan. It was just the three of us—and then it was the four of us. It was amazing. Here was this ugly little creature wrapped in my arms, and he was a mess and it was getting all over my shirt, and I was trying to wrap him in a blanket and I felt so awkward. I was torn between him and Joan, who still needed me, and the doctor kept telling me to do this and that. It was an instant I'd been prepared for, but when the baby came the feeling was so much stronger. It was just overwhelming. I cried. I let tears out and didn't feel ashamed about them at all.

I'm surprised at how many people I see who are still totally unaware of their feelings. I've noticed it in men I work with offshore. I would have thought things were changing faster. *I* changed a lot. Somewhere along the way I was able to release myself from the things that inhibit my father. It's a result of the times, I think, the total upheaval of the late sixties. I was caught up in that, and I was able to reexamine all sorts of things, and that was really the biggest rebellion I had against my parents—well, not against them, against what made them. They're products of the Depression. It must have been terrible growing up then. It must have created these very single-minded people who said, "I'm not going to let *this* happen to *my* family." That's the feeling I get from my father—this determination, this goal-achieving, like a crucible or something. Then as an adult he was thrown into World War II, which must have been rough, and it's made him the man he is—

uptight and determined—whereas he provided me the leisure and luxury to reexamine everything. I've made use of it. We discuss it, my father and I. He doesn't agree with me 90 percent of the time, but I think he's interested in seeing me explore it.

I hope not to make things too easy for Jason. I missed out on a lot of experiences, growing up fairly affluently. You know, when you go out camping you don't need all that fancy equipment.

I believe that you do not learn as much from another person's experience as you do from your own. That was one thing I liked so much about that summer with my father. He was an excellent craftsman and mechanic, but he had never taught me what he knew. He worked on cars, he built things in his machine shop, he did all sorts of things around the house, but he never let *me* do them. Sometimes he would *show* me, he would let me sit and watch, but I needed to actually hold the hammer in my hand and *do* it. He should have let me make the mistakes—that's the only way you learn. That's the thing I missed most. I felt I led too privileged a life, in a way. It was great that summer with my father—smashing my thumb with a hammer, learning how to build a house. I mean, the two of us built *the whole house.* A number of times afterward, when I was on my own, I made a living as a carpenter from what I learned.

I'm letting my son Jason do these things. Last weekend I was working out in the backyard, and he ruined a piece of wood I was working on. I had gone inside, and when I came back out I found he had taken some nails and a pot of glue and turned it over and made a terrible mess. But he thought he was doing what *I* was doing. He'd been watching me and he was copying me. So I didn't get mad at him. I just explained to him what he'd done wrong. He had the hammer and he was pounding on my piece of wood and splashing the glue around, but that's what he needs to do. My father was so efficiency minded. He wanted to do the most he could, and he had me just following behind him when I was a youngster. I wasn't as good at things as he was, so he would do all the work, whereas I'm willing to slow down a little for my son.

I love fatherhood. I started preparing myself for having a child when I was twenty-one, even though I didn't have Jason until I was twenty-eight. I had a collection of child-rearing books when I was in the army, and I read them all. It was important to me, I guess because I felt somehow sort of cheated. I wanted to correct that; I didn't want to continue the mistakes. I think what happens is that a parent teaches a child, the child becomes a parent and teaches the same thing, and it just keeps repeating. I was trying to change that. I remember consciously wanting to be more emotionally involved—or just more involved, period—with my child. I had scads of time in the army, and I read *The Feminine Mystique* and then I started reading child-rearing books. I knew that I wanted to have a child and I knew that I wanted to do it right.

Being a parent means a lot to me. It was really rough at first, however. I guess I had an idealized view of what it would be like; I had all the parts down about stimulating their minds and motivating them and loving them, but I didn't know at all about changing diapers or potty training or about when they're sick and throwing up. I didn't know how to deal with that. There were times when I thought, Oh, I'm not ready for this! Wait a minute! The positive aspects far outweigh the negative ones, but I do recognize that the negatives are there.

It's affected my marriage, for instance—just the lack of privacy. The baby came between us and was very much an intrusion. I tell myself now that it would have been a lot better if we had lived near our parents; we could have left him with them sometimes and not felt guilty about it. We always felt kind of guilty about baby-sitters, so we rarely got any relief. I have some anger at myself, and at my wife, for not managing better. My father probably would have been able to manage it, to cope with it. Gradually Jason began demanding more and more time, and there was no way I could have a child and not spend time with him. So I had to start pulling away from other things. I'd always closely guarded my private time. I

31

like to be by myself and not only part of a couple, and in the early morning I would read or write or just sit. I had to subtract from that time to give to Jason and also still give time to being a couple.

I'm finding already that Jason needs me less to do things for him, and yet it's my own desire to spend more time with him—talking, reading, doing things that are stimulating. I sense that he draws everything in. He's just like a sponge. I feel a challenge from that, and I want to give him as much as I can. I want him to learn to be careful of his emotions, to not shut them in, to be able to talk about what he's feeling and have an inquisitive mind. I'd like to have another child. I think I'd probably like to have a girl this time, but when Jason was born, it didn't matter. I just wanted a child.

One of the greatest joys to me is watching this little person become a person: watching him playing and pretending; watching his eyes roll around with all that curiosity; watching him ruin a piece of my wood; watching him on the river, walking down the levee off in his own little world.

3

William Lewis is a robust, country-reared Southwesterner whose powerful physique contradicts his inordinate gentleness. Mr. Lewis, forty-nine, works for a utility company in a major metropolitan area and commutes to and from his home in a rural community where he lives with his wife and son, Michael, a lanky fourteen-year-old edging six feet, his stepdaughter and two grandchildren.

I came from a lower-middle-class background, and I remember the meanest guy in our neighborhood, up until he was about seventeen or eighteen, would kiss his dad good-bye every time he'd go someplace. Nobody would dare say anything about it, because he'd *kill* you if you did. His dad was a massive, masculine man—he was about six feet three inches and must have weighed 300 pounds—and his uncle was a professional boxer. The whole family was very macho, including this boy. But of all the kids I knew, he showed the most affection for his dad. Nobody else I knew would kiss their dad when they said good-bye. I wasn't embarrassed by it; no, I was perhaps envious of his courage to do it.

I was pretty close to my father, and he included the whole family in just about anything he did. A lot of things he'd do might not be too interesting to us, but we'd still go along. If he was going hunting, for example, we'd all go with him. My father loved his family, and showed it. The best I could tell, he showed it the same way other parents showed it—you have to measure everything by the times. He'd kiss his wife once in a while, and maybe put his arm around my brother and me once in a while, especially if we did something he was proud of, like coming home with an *A* or winning a baseball game.

I've got my own ideas of what a father should be. I guess I do a lot of the same things my father did, although I didn't try to copy him—you just get influenced. One of the main things a son needs is discipline. Small punishments and small rewards mean a lot to a child. You take an eighteen-month-old baby, all you have to do is lightly tap his hand and the tears will flow. By the same token, if you say to a child, "Oh, that's great, you brought me the paper," well, he'll go get the paper for the next month because he's pleased you and you've let him know. I made it a point when my son was very young to reward him for the favorable things.

A child has also got to know he's loved. I recall when my son was about five, I had to get on to him for playing out in the middle of the street. I went over to him and said, "You *know* you're supposed to stay out of the street," and boy, he took off running into the house. I felt he needed to be shown that he'd done something wrong, so I went in and spanked him. When I got through and he was all upset, I told him I loved him and I put my arm around him. I let him know that the punishment was for something he'd done that was not the proper thing, and that it didn't have anything to do with my love for him or anything.

I don't think I would have been any different with a daughter, but I don't know because let's face it—boys and girls are still different in our society, whether we like it or not. It takes a while for things to really change; you can't just make a 180-degree turn. I could raise my son to where he would cook and marry a woman who would go out and make the living while he stayed home, but he would have a hard time in life. I feel you need to guide them down more or less traditional roads. Now, I will wash dishes, but not very often. When I do, I make my son help. I explain that he'll have to wash them if he lives by himself, or if he gets married and his wife is not around, or if his wife just wants him to help. There's no reason why he can't do it. By the same token, if I had a girl I'd want her to know how to fix a flat on a car, although it's not the normal thing she's going to be doing.

I really don't think what you see today, with fathers getting involved in their children's lives, is necessarily a change. You go back 100 or 150 years, fathers quite often delivered kids, and I'm sure they changed diapers. I think fathers have always been concerned with their wives' pregnancies, and have always felt tenderness toward their sons—well, always is an awful long time ago, but I'm sure they have. So it's probably not that things have changed that much, it's just that we're a more open society, so it seems new.

I don't know if I'd have wanted anything different with my father. I'm pretty well satisfied with the way our relationship was. Oh, we can all try to improve things, I guess. When somebody dies, people will say, "Gee, I wish I hadn't been mean to Joe yesterday 'cause he's dead today." I'd hate to have to say, "Doggone, I sure wish I'd done this or that for my son." I think you should do anything you can while you can do it. For example, today, when I get home I'm going to get my boy and take him into town to get him a baseball glove because he lost his old one. I think he's paid the price for losing it, and we've discussed it. He's been saving his allowance to get a new one, and I'm going to get it because I told him I would. I try to live up to my word with him. I recall being disappointed by my parents a couple of times when I was told they were going to do something, and then they never did it. I'm sure there were financial reasons, because times were hard. I might have overreacted but I probably try a little bit harder with my son because I remember that.

I think the most important elements in a relationship between a father and son are love, closeness and understanding. Understanding is a big thing. A child should be regarded as an individual. You have to ask yourself: Do I want him to play basketball because it's going to make *me* feel good, or because it's good for *him*? If a boy is five feet tall, he's not going to be a basketball player, so why go out and beat him to death because *you're* a frustrated basketball player?

Another thing is that a son, or a child, must be given independence. In many families he isn't allowed to grow up because a parent thinks, When he walks out of this house and gets married, then I'm old, but as long as he is my little baby, then I'm still young. One thing a parent ought to be shooting for all the time is to let the child grow up. Raising a child to be independent, to take care of himself, is an obligation that goes along with the fact that you have *had* the child in the first place. The day a child leaves and takes care of himself should be a proud moment.

Almost every time my father goes someplace, except to work, I can go with him if I want to [says Michael Lewis]. He takes me swimming and to play miniature golf or bowling. We do a lot of things together. He spends a lot of time with me when he gets home, and on weekends especially. I can talk to him about almost everything, about troubles in school and stuff like that. He's usually calm. And when he comes in, he kisses all of us. It makes me feel like he loves me a lot. Several kids in my class are downright bullies, and I don't think their fathers do that with them. It gives me security that my father's affectionate. It makes me feel like things are gonna be okay. I give it back to him, too. I expect I'll be the same when I have kids—hopefully even a little bit better. I'd try to be at home a little bit earlier, and I'd spend more time with them. Just be with them like my father is with me. Only a little more. He's one of the most perfect fathers, I think. He's kind, and he's usually never in a bad mood around me. If he wasn't this way, I'd probably be . . . I don't know, meaner.

If I do something wrong he usually just talks to me about it calmly. The last spanking I can remember him giving me was when I was six years old. It was for going out in the street. It made me feel sad at first because I thought he didn't love me. Later I realized he whipped me because he *did* love me. He wasn't even mad, just sort of disgusted I guess. I think fathers *should* discipline kids, 'cause if they don't they'll get in trouble almost all the time. I know one boy like that, and he's in the principal's office four times a week. I don't know what his father's like, but this boy is usually by himself and he wears ragged clothes—he's just a rebel.

My father's a little different than my mother with discipline. He talks and she spanks. Or sometimes she just gets fed up. I'm closer to my father. He spends more time with me. My sister and her two kids live with us, and there are a whole lot of other grandchildren, so during the daytime my mother has to watch the kids and stuff like that. My father is also a little more affectionate than my mother. I really do love my father. I guess I'm not affectionate with him in front of everybody—in front of real good friends, yes, but some people, no, because they'd go and tell *their* friends and then they'd start telling everybody in school to embarrass me, saying "He loves his father," and all that, and saying I'm gay. I know some kids who do that. Some people are that way, but it wouldn't stop me.

I'd say when I was young my dad and my mom shared about equally taking care of me. There were so many kids. I think I got closer to him when I got older. He takes me to do more things and he just spends more time with me. He's my friend.

I think it's a good idea that fathers today get more involved. It gives their kids more security and it makes them think that not just their mother loves them, but their father, too. When I'm a father I'll try to share pretty equally with my wife. The only thing a mother can do that a father can't is maybe spend more time with the kids if he works and she doesn't.

I think masculine would mean being kind to kids—not bossing them around. Men who say, "Do this!" or who beat their kids may think they're Mr. Big Shot. But I think kindness is more masculine.

4

The fifty-two-year-old publisher of one of the country's oldest and most reputable magazines, Town & Country, *David McCann, is the father of three teenagers, two sons and a daughter. Born in New York City, he lives with his family in Huntington, Long Island. He was interviewed in his Fifth Avenue office.*

I really have only fond memories of my father. I especially remember the last conversation I had with him. He was dying, although I didn't know it then. We were talking on the phone, and he asked how I thought my younger brother was doing, and he went on and on asking about him. I realized after my father died that he was getting his ducks in a row. He felt that my sister and I were on the way to success or happiness or whatever, but he wasn't sure about my brother and he wanted to settle his mind. That, I think, is the fondest memory I have of him, I guess because it was the most obvious sign that he really loved us.

My father was not the buddy type, not at all. He was a very introverted man, but he was a very *good* father and we were dependent on him for everything. My mother was the anchor in the house because when we were little she was the one who took care of us. We had household help so that she didn't have to do any of the chores, and we were with her all the time when we were little. My father was a lawyer, and very busy. If we confided in anybody, it was always my mother. She was the catalyst for everything. My father's indirect influence was that he was a very good man. I never heard him get angry; I never heard him use a coarse or vulgar word—never. I can remember my mother had to restrain him when we went to see *Kiss Me Kate.* The opening line when Kate came in was "You bastard!" Well, he was ready to get up and leave the theater. The way we were brought up, you simply did not use four-letter words. But it was part of the whole mystique of being Irish Catholic, too. As I perceived it, Irish Catholic families had a kind of formal upbringing, and the mother was the strong person who held the whole family together.

Because I could talk to my mother, she was much more of a person to me. I suppose I *could* have talked to my father too—I just never did. It wasn't that he was a fearsome person. It was just that my relationship with my mother was a closer one, and I think that's true in my family today. I'm out of the house so much, and my wife is there with the children when they're home.

I have a different relationship with my sons, I think, than my father did with my brother and me—and a similar one, too, in that I expect that my wife will play the same role my mother did with us. I expect it because I am away so much of the day and because I don't have dinner with the family. They have dinner at six o'clock, and I am not home by that time. It is different in that I am more of a buddy with my sons. I kid around with the younger one a lot, which my father didn't do. I was always close to my father but we were not buddies. And that is fine as far as father-son relationships go. You can't *be* a buddy to someone of a different generation, to begin with. Children must have an anchor, and a parent has to maintain that posture with them. If you come down to their level, if you try to be a peer, then they're lost.

There also have to be roots. There *have* to be. That was the way I was brought up, relatives in and out of the house all the time. On Sundays when I was a kid we would look out the window as a car would pull up and my father's sisters, who had never married, would be coming for a visit. That happened all the time. Some relative would arrive unannounced and everybody was happy to see everybody else. I feel that family is extremely important—it really is *everything*.

Both my sons are in athletics, and my wife used to think it was terrible that I wouldn't go and watch them play. But I couldn't, I just couldn't. I remember going to a hockey match when my younger son was goalie. He was just a little kid, nine years old, and he missed a puck as it came toward him and the opposing team got a goal. He just sat on the ice and cried, and I thought to myself, I can't stand it. I am never coming to one of these things again. I couldn't bear to see him cry. He was so upset that he had let this goal past him, and his sadness just tore me up. I started to cry myself. I don't believe in this Little League father-son thing. I think the Little League is fine, but those parents who go and push their kids to win are crazy. The one thing about the club we belong to, where the kids play sports, is that the attitude is one of playing the game. If you play and win, that's great. If you lose, that's okay too. Playing is what counts.

One thing I am absolutely certain of: my three children are all good. They are polite and kind—not only to animals and old ladies, but to everybody—and I don't think they would consciously hurt *anybody*. I think that if there is anything a parent wants from a child, that's number one. When I close my eyes, I could be at peace knowing my children were good people. Then I know my job has been accomplished.

My father was a very good man, too. I think he was probably one of the most saintly persons that I ever met. He gave himself—not just money, but *himself*—to charitable works. He was just a wonderful human being, and everybody knew it. I know that my brother and sister and I are what we are as a result of that, though none of us come even *close* to him in our behavior.

My father died in 1962, at age sixty. I was in my early thirties. I

45

can remember visiting him in the hospital. He was sitting on the bed being examined. I looked at him sitting on that bed and he looked like a . . . he looked like a little boy. And I was shocked— well, not shocked, exactly, but that was the first time I ever really realized he was another human being like anyone else.

I always knew all my life that my father loved me because he was *there*. I knew that if I needed him, he was there, and he would help me. That in itself is an expression of love. There was just never any doubt in my mind. I am much more absent in my children's lives than he was in mine. I suppose I am more selfish than my father in that I really am doing what I want to do. I *couldn't* work in Huntington. I have to be in New York and I have to be doing what I'm doing because that's what satisfies me. So I am something of an absent father—that's typical of our society, it seems—but I hope my children would say the same thing about me as a father that I have just said about *my* father: that they know I'm always there, whether physically or not. I couldn't care less whether they think of me as a man with a successful career. I think it's *nice* that the kids think it's just terrific to see my name in *Town & Country* every month. The cachet of being able to say, "My father is this or that," is great, but not as important as the basics. And the basics are these: I hope they can say, "I know my father loves me and I can always lean on him if I have to."

5

Fifty-six-year-old Weldon King, known locally as "Tunney," is as physically sturdy as the white pines in the wilderness of northern Maine. In his strong Maine dialect, while surrounded by the forests, crisp breezes and clear sunlight, he talks of the challenges he has mastered as a woodsman. He talks with tenderness and passion about this environment in which he was born and raised as was his father and now his own son. His twenty-four-year-old son "Tunney, Jr." is an outgoing happy-go-lucky person who enjoys the recognition his father worked so hard to achieve. In spite of their different views about their relationship, there is mutual respect and love.

My father was a beaver trapper and he ran a sporting camp, the Moose River Lodge, up on Lake Gilbert. There were twelve children in the family, five boys and seven girls. I was the first boy and fourth child. I thought my father was one of the best. We had a terrific relationship. I worked with him from the time I was seven or eight years old; I followed him like a little dog. Everything he did, I did. We were always together. In fact, I trapped beaver with him four or five winters in the woods. I was just a little young fellow. I would get out of school and I would have to make up my studies in the spring. He was a terrific hunter and fisherman and he loved it right up until he died. He was probably about as good a fly fisherman as you could find.

I admired him for this reason: he always let me voice my opinion. We had a farm, too, and I worked with him taking care of hay and cows and so forth. He wasn't a bossy type guy saying, "You better do this, you better do that." He was the type that would ask, "Well, what should we do today?" I don't think I ever had a hard word with my father in all my life. I really thought the world of him. In my eyes there was no better father. My mother was the one that did most of the scolding. She was very stern. My father was kind of an easygoing person. Oh, I respected him. I wouldn't cross him or anything like that. He was a very affectionate man. He used to go swimming with us and teach us things and sing to us. He was very unusual. He loved children. I think that was it. In those days most fathers were more strict and stern, more so than they are today. I've done the same thing with young Tunney. We have a very good relationship, very good. In fact, we never have *any* problems. He's been going with me in the woods since he was three years old. I do about the same thing with him my father did with me. If we're gonna do something I always ask his opinion of it.

My father was a real strong, powerful man. He weighed 225 pounds. He was a real rugged man, but he was very affectionate. I always looked up to him. I can't say one thing bad about him.

I was competitive and he was too. I would work with him and try to keep up with him and do things like that but as far as me feeling that he *thought* different, no. I was the type that if I was working I'd go right at it. In fact I worked with him in the woods all winter when I was thirteen. I enjoyed working with him. He was reasonable; he wasn't a father that would push you around and scold you and holler at you. I don't think he ever hollered at me in my life.

I wouldn't want our relationship changed in any way. I was perfectly happy. I think back all the time, I go back over the years and think of the way I was brought up, and I loved every minute of it. He was very affectionate with me even when I was in my teens. He would brag me up, telling me I was a good man. I could tell that he loved me and that he thought a lot of me. He would never down me on anything. It helped me, no doubt; there's no question about it. And I think it's made me the same way, too, because I feel I do the same things with young Tunney.

Tunney was with me constantly. He's been with me since he was old enough to go into the woods. 'Course it made it hard for me because I was more or less a baby-sitter. I'd take him in the woods and then I'd have to watch him because I had a lot of equipment running. Years ago, probably when I first got started in 1946, I wouldn't have been able to do that. By the time Tunney was three or four I had quite a crew in the woods. I had a foreman so I didn't have to get involved in the work itself.

My own personal feeling is that more fathers should do like I've done with my son and my father did with me—spend a lot of time with your boy. I like the idea that fathers are doing more of this now. I'm very affectionate with babies, myself. I can take a baby and rock him for hours, you know. I love kids.

I have two daughters, nineteen and twenty-one. I enjoy my daughters very much—in a different way, of course. I realize the difference between boys and girls and that there are things Tunney and I do that the girls more or less *don't* do. I enjoy playing tennis and going out in a boat, riding and things like that. If my daughters wanted to get involved in the business, that would be all right. I know a couple of ladies whose husbands died and they're still running the business and they're very good. There's no reason why my daughters can't do it.

I think that a father who ignores his children is doing wrong. They're going to have a poor relationship. I wouldn't have had a good relationship with my father if he'd ignored me. Fathers don't have to be tough with their sons. I'm very mild with Tunney.

I was brought up in a big family, a poor family, but it was wonderful. At that time everybody had to work hard to survive because it was the Depression. I've done very well, which has made me a lot easier with Tunney. I don't want him to do the kind of work I had to do. In those days, everybody worked hard. I used to get up at three or four in the morning and feed horses when I was twelve years old and be gone all day and think nothing of it. But I wouldn't want Tunney doing that. In the period when I was between say twelve to nineteen I didn't get to go out and play ball and do things because I was too busy working. You're only young once and I want Tunney to enjoy it.

My father and I get along fine [says Tunney, Jr.]. Sometimes we don't but most of the time we understand each other. He can kid around with me. Most of the time we can talk. We've had our differences. I'm a little rebellious at times, but I suppose everybody goes through that: Your father doesn't want you to do something and you want to be with the crowd or whatever. He's not really that affectionate. He's not one to come up and give me a hug or kiss and tell me he loves me, but I know he does. He wants to make sure I'm happy all the time. He lets me know that if there's anything I want I should ask him, and if it's possible for him to give it to me he will. He always makes sure that I'm doing things that he hasn't done before. He wants me to have the things he never had. Like giving me a boat or sending me to a friend's graduation party or something like that, just really extravagant. He wouldn't do the things he does for me if he didn't love me.

Maybe he was affectionate when I was little. Now when I sit and talk to him, I can tell there's affection there, but he's not one to show it. If he put his arm around me, I'd feel pretty good about it. It's just a form of greeting or . . . or affection, that shows you care for somebody.

Dad's pretty low key. He likes to take things as they come, and if something arises he faces the problem head on. He doesn't put any demands on me. If I want to go someplace, do something different, it's fine with him. He just wants to see the best for me.

Sometimes I feel pressure because he's done well in his business. I don't know whether I want to continue in his footsteps or try something else, like hotel work. I like working with people and my father is not a "people person." He'd rather sit home and look out at Mount Kineo. I'd like to continue in his business because I can see what potential the logging business has, and I like the woods and I like this area. He'd be tickled pink if I did. Oh, God, no, he wouldn't reject me if I didn't. He wants to see the best for me. Whatever I decide to do, he'll stand behind me 100 percent.

I hope I can do half as well as he's done, then I'd feel I had accomplished quite a bit. But I don't feel I *have* to live up to it, no. I told him I was not taking a forestry course and he didn't seem too upset about it.

If I have a son I'll probably spend a little bit more time with him when he's younger. I spent a lot of time with my father before I went to school. He used to take me into the woods when I was three years old. I'd get up at three o'clock in the morning and do things with him. But I'd spend more time doing stuff with my kids. I know this guy who's got two beautiful kids and they're sharp as tacks. He does *everything* with them. He devotes almost his whole life to those kids, and they're really well rounded and adjusted. Both parents should spend an equal amount of time. And if I have kids I'm going to let them do what they feel they want to do in their hearts. If they don't feel right doing something, then they can do something else. Sometimes my father wants me to do what he wants me to do.

6

W. C. Mueller and his thirteen-year-old son Bill were interviewed on a commercial airplane as they returned from a weekend hunting trip on the Gulf Coast to their home city of Dallas. Bill is an alert-eyed, inquisitive eighth grader; Mr. Mueller, a business executive for a radio company, is also the father of another son, aged nine.

I'm close to my father [says Bill Mueller]. I like a lot of the things he likes: messing around with radios, flying, hunting. This weekend he took me hunting for the first time. It was really fun. We've been spending more time with each other than we used to, because we do the same things, we have the same interests. We have six cars, and he takes me out in his Corvette sometimes. He also likes taking me flying and stuff like that.

I think fathers are different from mothers because they usually have the same interests as boys. But my mother is more affectionate. A good father has to care about a son and do things like go out in a field and play baseball. A bad father doesn't care about his children or he spoils his children. He just lets them do what they want. Sometimes my father loses his temper with me when I do something wrong, but it's understandable. When a kid does something bad, the father should tell him about it and maybe send him to his room for a while to think about it.

I don't see my father a lot. Well, I see him on weekends, but he works a lot and sometimes he's in Japan for a month. When he comes home from work we eat and then he usually stays in his room and watches TV or works on papers. He has a tough job. It's not that great like this, because when we don't see each other we don't share our opinions or stuff like that. If I could change anything, the only thing I can think of is to be with him a lot more. When he's home at night watching TV, I'll walk in and out all the time just to see how he's doing. And if he calls me in for something, I'll go running.

I liked it when we went hunting. Like this morning, sitting in a duck blind by ourselves where it was cold, the wind was blowing, there was no roof, just sitting there looking around, trying to be quiet. We talked a little bit about a movie I saw and he was asking me how it ended, and we just talked about things while we waited. It was nice being alone and being quiet with nothing but the wind and cold. It makes you feel real close.

I'm relatively busy [says W.C. Mueller]. I'm a little bit of a workaholic and I do a fair amount of traveling, so I spend whatever time I can—and a little more than I think I can—with my two boys. I like to teach them things, and work with them on science projects and various assignments. On a daily basis I probably average an hour and a half with them, except on special occasions like this hunting trip where I spent four days with Bill. Personally I think my wife should also spend a little more time with them.

I'd like to make more time available to them, particularly at the ages they are now. In fact, I'm making career adjustments so I can do that. Sometimes I'll take them to the office and they'll help out with chores or work, with me doing experiments and so forth.

I think the father is more the authority figure and should be able to spend time with his children in their earlier stages. But this should be shared by both parents. I was pretty close to my father, although he didn't spend a great deal of time with me. He was

German born and did not have a naturally forthcoming kind of attitude, not nearly as much as I do with my boys. However, I didn't resent it because Dad and I were close. We got along very well.

Being a father is miraculous. It's a common miracle, but it's one of the most valuable, rewarding experiences you can ever have. The heartaches may be frequent, but the joys are substantial.

7

Psychiatrist Nicholas Ward, thirty-two, who grew up in New Jersey and attended medical school at Cornell, practices in Seattle, Washington. He is the conscientiously involved father of a three-year-old son and nine-month-old daughter.

For me, being a father is a very positive thing. I certainly don't see it as competitive. That's not *my* role. Certainly there's an analytic theory that fathers and sons are in the death throes of competition. I think that's a popular view of the relationship but I'm not sure it happens all the time, or even frequently. And when I look at my own friends or family, I don't see any of that. Competition is surely a very small part of the father-son relationship, and often isn't obvious at all.

I think the Freudian view is that it's an actual competition, and the popular view is that the father's relationship with the son is less tender, less warm and more of an "I'll teach you this" nature—he's a teacher of skills rather than a provider of emotional needs.

When I look at my friends, or my own situation or even at my brothers, there's certainly a trend away from the father as just skill-giver, to the father meeting the emotional needs of a child. Most of my friends see themselves very much in the role of being good, loving parents.

Along with the flower-child revolution that supposedly failed there has been a trend, at least in the under-thirty-five age group, of men feeling more comfortable about showing their feeling or responsibility to children and family. Interestingly, I've seen it sometimes come together and sometimes not, where the father isn't particularly warm but feels a responsibility that he *should* be more involved. In the happy circumstances where it does come together, the father feels he's important and that he can meet the children's emotional needs.

I think there's something very interesting that happened to certain fathers among my friends. They wanted to participate and their wives wouldn't let them. It was the first child, and the mothers got into the mothering experience very deeply. They did the childbirth preparation thing, they made sure the bonding was just right, they knew that breast feeding was going to be wonderful. But I've seen some mothers who are so bonded with their babies that it was clear there wasn't much room for the father unless he was quite aggressive about taking care of the child. It seemed especially true with the breast-feeding mothers.

I feel quite actively involved with my children. My wife and I went through childbirth preparation together. There was a high chance of her being delivered by C-section, with a 9½ pound baby in breech position, and indeed it came to that. I was there, and what was remarkable was that I experienced everything that had been written about bonding: an instantaneous elation and love. All this intellectual stuff about competitive sons was out the window.

I'm a psychiatrist and I look at things rationally, logically, in words, and most of what I experienced doesn't verbalize very well. I can't find words to characterize what fatherhood was like. I could tell people about dirty diapers and stuff, but I had a very hard time talking about, "That's my son, he's precious to me, it's a special thing, I feel a great deal of love for him." It's not like the love for my wife; in some ways it's stronger, less conditional. I tried writing poetry about it, because I had published as a poet, and found myself somewhat lacking for words. One of the images that came to mind was that he was hinged to my soul, that there were strings going right back and through me.

I've never thought along Jungian lines before, but I certainly do now. This bonding to your child, this feeling that you'll take care of it, is a basic thing in the human race that goes way beyond words. I must admit that my wife was much more bonded to our son before he was born; to me it was still just an interesting idea. I remember Jean shared her room with a woman who'd had her child the day before, and it just seemed totally unbelievable that the next day we would be in exactly the same situation.

Definitely I had trepidations about having a child. I was thirty when Gaylin was born and my wife was thirty-two. I was used to living all of my adult life without a child around, and I was really worried about what it would mean in terms of being able to do anything, to have any freedom. I was worried particularly that I wouldn't have those feelings that I've been talking about, so that it would really seem like total drudgery. But it didn't turn out that way.

Most of what my wife and I talk about now are the children, whereas before we talked more about what we were doing or our relationship. I even talk less about my job—partly out of guilt. I come home and if there's something exciting that's happened at work, that's sometimes the last thing Jean wants to hear. She's staying home with the children, but it was a very conscious decision on her part to do so. She'd been a psychiatric social worker and had worked for sixteen years, so she didn't feel like she was going to lose the identity she had realized in her career. She was actually looking forward to being home. But I felt I shouldn't look too excited or happy about what was happening at work, that I should keep it more to myself than I used to.

Because my wife had a C-section, she couldn't lift Gaylin in the beginning, so I was exclusively the one that got up at night to bring the baby over to her, and I would diaper him and so forth. On weekends or evenings it was about a 70/30 split, with me doing 70 percent. As it turned out, the first two words my son put together were, "Daddy, bottle." That was his first command, and he asked me, not her. I had real mixed feelings: "Gosh, I'm the important one," but also "Why is it four in the morning, and why did I get into this?" I was feeling very ambivalent—the feeling of importance and the drudgery. An interesting thing about Gaylin is that he alternates in his loyalties to us, but more often we will see that he's Daddy's boy. And that means that if one of us is going to change his diaper, he'll say, "Daddy do it." Then he'll go on for two weeks or a month saying, "Mommy do it." So it's not exclusive by any means. When there's an adult couple around, he'll immediately approach the male first with the expectation that the male is going to pick him up and hold him. Not that he's negative toward females—he just usually approaches the male first. I don't know if it's standard with kids, but he almost always puts on my clothes or my shoes when he plays dressing up.

In a lot of literature, they talk about the mother being there for the child, meeting emotional needs, et cetera, but the father providing the excitement and play. I think that's true to a point, based on how long you end up taking care of them. On the evenings when I have energy, I throw him up and down because Jean just can't do it; she's not strong enough now or is too tired after a day with him. But if I have him all day on the weekend, my style becomes very much more like hers. I'll say, "You can sit on my lap, but I think I want to watch the TV right now," or "Let's listen to music." I'm less active with him. In that way I approximate more what's called mother style. I think it has something to do with how long you're with a child at any given time.

In my family we had a positive relationship with our father, but I was the youngest of five boys. My father was more of a stereotypical father in that he would play football with us and teach us math and that sort of thing. He would teach us skills. I don't know if he ever cuddled my brothers when they were younger. He seemed to like to play with three- and four-year-olds, drawing pictures for them and that sort of thing. I decided, and one of my older brothers did also, that we weren't going to be like that; we were going to give more emotional support and have more interaction. It was a conscious decision on both our parts that we'd try to be there more often, and if not there more often, at least actively supporting what the child was doing.

Something like thirty minutes a week is the average a father spends with a child giving him exclusive attention. That's a statistic often quoted now. I think spending time is important. "Quality" time is a lot of crap. My own rhythm is that I'm better in the morning, and I kind of run out of steam as the day goes on, so that when I come home in the evening I'm not giving the quality of time I can give in the morning. Even to call it quality time is a folly. A working woman I would assume would have a similar experience. So I think you have to be with a kid at a variety of different times.

I would definitely have liked more time with my father. Of course, being the fifth of five sons, I had four surrogate fathers. They often took over and I had more interactive time because of them. I'm sure that's where I got a lot of emotional needs met. I remember very vividly the closest I ever felt to my father was when he came down with hepatitis. He had to stay home in bed for a couple of months. I was in second grade and I felt very close to him. He taught me four grades of math and four grades of English so that I didn't have to do homework or think about my schooling for a while. I learned so much faster from him, and it was so much more important. I also felt he was physically getting more tired by the time I came along. He played more athletics with my brothers. He wrestled with my two oldest brothers and he never did that with me. The few times he did do athletic things with me, it really stood out: Gosh, he came out and threw the football with me. Obviously, it was symbolically important. He was paying special, exclusive attention to something I was doing in a positive way.

Sometimes I've wanted to show a closer relationship to my father but I always felt that I wanted him to make the first move, and it never happened. That, I think, is a societal thing. Fathers very rarely say, "I love you," or "Boy, you're really neat and I like you a lot." I say it to my three-year-old and I wonder, will I still say it to him when he's twelve years old, or will I feel constrained that I shouldn't say it or that I shouldn't hug him? I hope not. But I am aware that those constraints are operating in my relationship with my father.

I've thought a lot about approaching my father, particularly in the early seventies. One of my special areas was group therapy, and it would often come up in the group: Why can't you get closer? And I would keep thinking about it and never do it. Then someone would say, "My father died and I wish I had done it," and I'd think Oh, my God. I can tell you that I intellectually feel it's good, but I never end up doing it. I'm not sure how he'll react. The other thing I'm aware of is that it's already happening on a nonverbal level. So that I don't know how much it would drastically change things except to confirm something.

In my experience with my good male friends, we never say, "I really like you." But there's an absolutely clear understanding communicated nonverbally that that's the case. I think a lot of male relationships are more often on a nonverbal level. Males don't necessarily talk a lot to one another but they do something together and show a closeness *that* way.

My father had a very domineering father who felt that he should be a certain class of student. He didn't think much about athletics. My father was an extremely good athlete—a gymnast, a football player, a wrestler, et cetera. He still holds a world record in an event that was cancelled after he broke it because it became lethal. It was the rope climb. My father did it by throwing his whole body up six feet at a time with his arm length. The guy who tried to beat him two months later died in the event and they decided it had become too dangerous. Anyway, my father said that only one time did his father came to watch him in athletic competition. Because of the way his father was in directing him academically, my father vowed that he would not be overly obtrusive in directing our lives. But it almost became a laissez-faire thing when I got accepted to Cornell. I was very excited and my father's approach was, "Now are you sure this is what you want to do?" He was following through on his philosophy that he would not show too much enthusiasm about the direction I was going because it might make me feel I *should* go in that direction. He backed off a lot from that, and I think maybe too far. I think what I'd want to do with Gaylin is show enthusiasm about what he does well, and if he somehow feels a subtle pressure, it will be a minor loss compared to the gain.

I guess the best part of fatherhood is the feeling that I get from it, the satisfaction, the love. There's a moving and a static part to it. The static part is the bonding that feels so good. The moving part is the growth; watching my son change and grow is really neat. I can't believe I'm saying this, but there have been stages that I kind of wished he hadn't gone through quite so fast. I'd like to slow his development down so I could enjoy that stage longer. My experience with the second child is probably less like that because I have less energy. She's moving right along through it, and at least for now that's fine.

One thing my wife noticed is that I bonded faster to my daughter than *she* did. She was hospitalized two weeks before delivery with a kidney infection and had terrible anemia. She was really sick by the time the baby came and had no energy left and I suspect that had something to do with it. She was also expecting a boy because there were only boys in my family. She realized only later that she was expecting sameness, that she would bond to another Gaylin. And when Joanna was born, she wasn't another Gaylin. She was a different human being. I was expecting difference so I think that made it easier for me.

I think I always wanted to be a father—if nothing else, just for the feeling of, "I'll do it better." One of the first courses I took was in child development. That intrigued me more than anything else. The thing I came away with was, no matter what society does, and no matter what it thinks priorities are, there can't be anything more important than the upbringing of the next generation. There just *can't* be.

8

Gerard Piel is the founder and publisher of Scientific American, *the most prestigious scientific magazine in the world. His son Jonathan, forty-two, a former writer for the American Institute of Physics and for* Newsweek, *is editor of* Scientific American Medicine. *The elder Mr. Piel had two sons by his first wife, a daughter by his second. Jonathan Piel is the father of two girls.*

I suppose I dodged into fatherhood innocently, because it was expected of me, just as I went through college because it was expected of me. I didn't ask many questions when I was younger. Certainly it was clear to me that I wasn't out to have six kids, but the idea of having children was wonderful, and I was very much involved in the raising of my two sons. Their mother and I worked out a sort of labor-sharing as well as pleasure-sharing relationship. Once the children were ambulatory and going to school, she joined the faculty. So she put in a pretty solid day of work as a teacher and mother.

I was very much involved in my career, working in a very competitive environment at Time Inc. in those early years, so my days with my children were Saturdays and Sundays, and those were always reserved for some kind of adventure—sledding, museums, going to the country, and going fishing.

My relationship with my father was a much more distant one.

The kind of thing I did with my kids was much less frequent with my father. He took an enormous interest in his kids, but he did it in kind of a secondary, ricochet way. He was a shy, bookish person. With four boys in the family, he became very much involved in the Boy Scouts, but on a large institutional basis. He set up a whole adult program to support scouting out in Nassau County, and he would sit down and write elaborate constitutions for the Scouts and marvelous sorts of rituals. It was very much through this sort of screen that he related to us.

He ran Piel Bros., the brewery, which his father and uncle founded, and he ran it all through the days of Prohibition. My grandfather did not believe that brewers should own saloons, so when Prohibition came in the Piels were not equipped with real estate as were other German brewing families who survived. We barely squeaked through the grim days of Prohibition and with repeal we walked into the grim days of the Depression. So the Piel family was not a rich family by any means.

I knew my father loved me—he was always interested in everything I had to say, and that relationship became warmer and warmer as I grew up. In the later years, in prep school and college, I would come home with a new bit of learning or a new set of ideas about the world and would have the most marvelous conversations with him. Then as I got on into making my own living, he would always want to hear everything I was doing, and when my mother died I was very much the member of the family who provided family support for him. This was all very warm, and he was thrilled to hear all the things I was doing as science editor of *Life* magazine. I shared with him a great passion for dry-fly fishing, and I'm happy to say I have his dry-fly rod today and still fish with it.

He was not competitive. On the contrary, it was "Oh, how marvelous that you're doing what you're doing." When I started *Scientific American* he just couldn't hear enough about it and would regale other people with the things I told him. Even though he was disappointed that I went off and did something else. That's a curious thing about the Piel family—no member of my generation went into the brewery.

I went to Catholic schools in Woodmere, Long Island, then to Brooklyn Preparatory School, a Jesuit school in Brooklyn to which I commuted with my father. That's another relationship we had. He would be reading the paper and I would be doing my homework as we took the train together in the morning. It was determined that I would go to Andover, mainly out of my mother's social ambitions for the family. She was bitterly disappointed; she had married a rich man and then with the collapse of the business she found herself married to a poor man. Nonetheless, she had high social ambitions for her children and sent us off to private schools.

Ours was a warm but somewhat distant relationship. He was very supportive. When I say distant, that's as compared to the close, supervisory, driving, rather negative relationship that all of us had with our mother. She was the one who established our ambitions and goaded us to succeed and *exceed,* whereas my father was happy with us the way we were—one had that feeling. He was warm and supportive and welcoming of just about *anything* we did. He was more verbally and histrionically demonstrative. He gave us enthusiastic and loud verbal response, but no horseplay. He wouldn't have *dreamed* of horseplay. I think I was closer to my children—there was *lots* of horseplay, touch football, wrestling with them. Hugging and kissing comes along with horsing and games.

I wish my father had been happy. He was a burdened man, carrying responsibility not only for his wife and children but for his mother and brothers and sisters, keeping the whole bloody thing afloat, and engaged in a line of work he didn't fancy much. His evenings at home would frequently be a retreat into reading. He was educated in late nineteenth-century classical literature, and knew Greek, Latin and German. He also wrote sort of grim poetry, epic and romantic and full of fantasy. So I could have had more involvement with him if he hadn't needed to get the tension out of his stomach muscles by being alone in the evening.

My son Sam was twenty-four years old when he died. Certainly it is the most unacceptable form of mortality. You know, you can't reconcile to that. You can to the deaths of parents and friends.

Jonathan was hired by the American Institute of Physics on a National Science Foundation grant to test the proposition that there could be new ways to launch a science story. Jonathan didn't have much qualification as a journalist but as he watched the stream of literature on its way to press, he could spot the story that ought to be reported to the wider public, get in touch with the author, and by the time the article appeared in print, have a soundly grounded press release ready to go out. He lived in our apartment on Central Park West, went to work every day, came home at night and hit the books, and by golly he was making the front page of the *New York Times* once a month, making the science column in *Time* and *Newsweek,* and really proving that he had a sound proposition. The science editor at *Newsweek* had the sense to ask, "Where the hell is this wonderful stuff coming from?" and hired Jonathan. At *Newsweek* he proceeded to do a first-rate job. What he's got that's part of his real native gift is the capacity to tell a story, to do a solid job of intellectual analysis of a manuscript, but to come out of it with a plot. And by my judgment he's the best editor of his generation we ever had on the magazine.

After he'd demonstrated what he could do as an editor, we decided we needed his talents—we *really* needed him. The style of promotion the magazine now has was established by Jonathan six or seven years ago. Then there came this marvelous opportunity to do something that's now called *Scientific American Medicine,* so that added the next big dimension to his experience and he's done that beautifully.

There's a curious element here. Johno sort of replaced his brother, who was a premed student, in medicine. I think the poetic aspect is something he's quite aware of, though I don't think that was the *motive*: it was the job that had to be done. And it's a success at this point. Nobody has any doubt about the quality of the work he's done.

He's an affectionate, concerned, attentive father who spends lots of time with his two little daughters, and they just adore him. There's very little sibling competition between these two kids because they both get so much love. He's really grand—a much better father than I was. I think he gives his kids more time and more love than I gave mine. I think I worked harder than Johno—I've been a workaholic ever since I can remember. Johno is much more of an employee. He does his job magnificently, and he doesn't need to do more than eight hours a day—so more power to him.

Jonathan has certainly had a sense of rivalry with me, and I don't think it's Freudian at all. He has felt that he had to succeed on account of my example or something. That's surely been tough on him. The tension between him and me has been all on the side of emulation, not competition, or of his having to prove himself. He's gone on to do so wonderfully, and it just grows all the time.

Before our first child was born [said Jonathan Piel] I had imagined that being a parent would be a really awesome responsibility that would somehow be a great weight, a responsibility that would be very difficult to carry out and would demand a kind of extraordinary continuous effort. I didn't see how anyone could ever do it. I don't know why I had that impression. As soon as Sarah was born, parenthood just seemed to be the most natural thing in the world. It's very funny, in so many ways it just seemed to fit right in with what I was able to do, and I discovered very quickly that it was a tremendous pleasure to be a parent. It was downright fun, which surprised me. Watching my daughter grow from a newborn infant to a ten-year-old on the threshold of what appears to be an increasingly early adolescence in our society, is great fun.

I think that in terms of formal knowledge I was totally unprepared for being a parent. I think most of us are. The mythologies that we absorb about childhood as we grow up, and what being a parent is like, are totally inaccurate and bear no relationship to the real experience. Perhaps it's a graver deficit in our acculturation than are the mythologies we pick up about sexuality; early infancy is described as like taking care of an F. A. O. Schwarz doll. One acquires all these clothes and gadgets and tools for taking care of the baby, and the baby is envisioned as passive, as psychologically pliant. Babies are nothing of the kind. They start out full of their own ideas of what they want, and it's like shooting the rapids from the word go. It never stops.

I'm very involved in raising our kids. My wife and I agree that it's something we both share and do together. In terms of the amount of time we spend, it's more her responsibility than mine, but I spend as much time as I can. I spend a lot of time with the kids on weekends, and a lot of time with them when I come home at night. We kind of take turns being the first out of bed in the morning to get breakfast. I'm very involved in their education and the decisions we make about it, so child rearing is something we share together. It's both intensely enjoyable and intensely annoying. I find that the time available to me to stay in touch with the adult world even on as simple a level as reading the newspaper in the morning has virtually disappeared, and that is tremendously irritating. When you don't have children, you have more freedom to organize your time the way you want. I think that's one of the things we don't learn about before we have children. On the other hand, the payoff of watching your child learn, grow, develop skills and capacities, is just tremendous. The other payoff is that the kid is a helluva lot of fun to be with.

No, I'm not disappointed in not having a son. We know people who have had three or four children until they manage to roll a Y instead of an X. If I wanted a son, I'd think twice about it just on the grounds that our hands are full with Sarah and Kate. I find myself thinking with some apprehension about the world they'll be moving into as young women. I see an awful lot of mistreatment and devaluation of women in the business and academic worlds and I am cynical enough to think an awful lot of that will be around when they become adults. That's a challenge they're going to have to confront. I would like to see those things change.

I don't really see my role as a father as different from my own father's except that my father spent relatively less time with me and my brother and sister than I do with my children. But the quality of the time he spent with us was as good, if not better, in some ways. He would take us out on sort of Sunday morning adventures. We'd go out for breakfast and then we'd go to a museum or we'd walk around parts of the city we'd never seen before or go out to the Statue of Liberty or up to the Cloisters or have some kind of a wonderful Sunday morning expedition. That was in part designed to let my mother sleep late, but mostly it was for us to have time together, and they were truly wonderful experiences.

We've always been a very physical family, in body contact with each other. I can remember sitting on my father's lap, roughhousing with him. We still hug when we haven't seen each other in a while. He was a very affectionate father when we were little kids. I never thought of it as unusual—I think of it as more unusual now that we're adults than I did when we were kids. I think affection makes for the opposite of sissies, in that one is comfortable with one's affectionate feelings and has the courage to express them. One is not afraid that hugging or kissing your father or brother or a good friend is sissy.

In terms of communicating values, Pop always did so on an adult level. Obviously the Sunday mornings and the close, enjoyable times we had together were communicating all kinds of values, and good ones. As far as being a disciplinarian is concerned, or giving us a sense of how we were supposed to behave as males, my father had very strong ideas about how we should behave with other people, with our peers. Fairness and kindness were two values he communicated to us. I remember specifically in Central Park one day when I was about ten—my brother was about nine—we were playing softball. We'd take our bat and ball and go pick up a game on a Sunday morning. I was captain of one of the two teams we formed. One of my players made a horrible defensive error, and about three runs got across the plate. I came screaming in from the outfield—really ripping this kid who'd fumbled the ball and let these runs come in. Pop reprimanded me quite sharply for talking that way to the other kid.

If I could have changed the relationship with my father, I'd like to have spent more time with him as I was growing up. The quantity of time was somewhat deficient, but I suppose many people feel that way. It was when Pop was starting the magazine and he really was awfully busy. And while he was starting the magazine, he also doing a lot of free-lance writing. What with putting us through school, paying the rent and doing something he loves very much, he didn't have much spare time. Those were the things I couldn't see as a kid, but I don't think I was resentful as much as I just wished we could be together more.

I think he always had very high expectations for his children— not usual expectations in terms of my-son-the-doctor or my-son-the-corporate-lawyer, but high expectations in the sense that he wanted us to make our lives count, the way he wanted to make his *own* life count. He has extremely high standards, and he also has the courage to live his life according to very strong values and principles, and he expects himself to live up to those principles. That's why he published *Scientific American* and why he's involved in all the things he's involved in. He expected me and my brother and sister to lead our lives in the same sort of way. My sister was born when I was twenty-one, so she wasn't part of my early childhood or adolescence. I see her going through the same kind of relationship in this sense with Pop that I went through. He put great pressures on us in many ways. I wondered if I was good enough to measure up to it, if I had the courage and intelligence and determination. He's a perfectionist, and when one is confronted with the standards of perfectionism it can make one judge oneself rather harshly. Sometimes. But resolving those feelings is part of the task of growing up.

I think in the back of my mind, I was always very interested in doing what Gerry is doing. His interest in science and technology and their impact on society kindled the same interests in me. It seemed like a particularly fascinating way to look at how human society works, and a fascinating leverage point for having some impact on how our society functions. The questions that scientists, biologists and psychologists ask about the world we live in and ourselves are intrinsically fascinating. Therefore, to be close to people who are working on those questions—to be able to look over the whole spectrum, enjoy all the exciting discourses—seemed like a great thing to do.

I went to a little school called City and Country down in Greenwich Village. Then I went to Putney, then Harvard, where I majored in history. My first job was at the American Institute of Physics—a general sort of service organization set up by the major physical societies in the United States. I worked in the public relations department writing press releases on significant work published in the journals. Then I got a job offer from *Newsweek*, which I grabbed. That was really what I wanted to be doing, writing and reporting. At the American Institute of Physics, I was writing and reporting, but it was in a sort of public relations atmosphere. At *Newsweek* I was what is known as a swing writer. I worked in science, medicine and education, but mostly in science and medicine doing feature stories, writing the department when the editor was on vacation, being the cleanup man on Saturday morning. It was a great place to work. Then I came to work here. It was something I always wanted to do, but I didn't want to just walk out of Harvard with freshman beanie on and start working for *Scientific American*. It was very important to me to prove to myself and to the people here that I could do an effective, competent job on the demanding level that is typical of *Scientific American.* So I wanted very much to win my spurs in the outside world—which is what I did.

I am in charge of *Scientific American Medicine,* which is a two-volume, loose-leaf advanced text for practicing physicians. It's been published for two years. It's a completely new venture we started four years ago. We have 20,000 subscribers and are still growing.

I would say that coming into an organization my father founded only enhances my identity. I've always loved *Scientific American* and I share the values and motives that led Gerry to found it. So I find it tremendously fulfilling to work here and be in charge of a venture that is making use of the editorial standards, policies and approaches of *Scientific American* for a slightly more rarefied population. I think my working here has largely affected our relationship positively. I'd almost like to cancel that answer because it's too pat, but what I mean is, I find it very fulfilling to work closely with Gerry. He's a very bright guy; he's got terrific ideas. I enjoy his sense of humor, and I find it awfully exciting to work with him. Another part of the answer is that I work very independently of him. I'm in charge of this venture, and I talk to him about what I'm doing every once in a while, but he's not breathing down my neck or looking over my shoulder telling me what shots to call. I sit down with him a few times a year and tell him what's happening, and he usually has good ideas and observations, which I find useful. I think I'd find it terribly stultifying if he were sitting on my shoulder, and he has much better things to do with his time. People will ask me, "Is Gerry in town this week?" and I'll say, "Search me." He travels so much. We have a series of national language editions of *Scientific American* —in Japan, China, Italy, Spain, Germany, France—so Gerry is constantly ricocheting around the world either working with publishers of those editions or on work indirectly related to *Scientific American.* He lives in his own time zone; he's not really around to be seen that much. So in terms of time and space I have a great deal of independence and I enjoy it.

He'd probably describe our relationship pretty much the same way. We enjoy working together, we enjoy each other's company. I disagree with him about some things, but he has an unnerving habit of usually being right. I've disagreed with him on political or social issues, and then I've watched how the game breaks down and a few months later I'll say, "My God, he was right."

My brother's death at twenty-four in some ways made Pop and me much closer emotionally in that we both shared a horrible, tragic loss. It was just one of those terrible, sudden things. In any event, because it was so awful and we both felt so deeply about it, it made us closer emotionally. It didn't change the tenor of our relationship or the way we were with each other, but somehow it made us closer.

My father didn't have favorites, certainly not in his objective loving of us. I think there may have been some temperamental ways in which my brother was closer to Pop than he is to me, was to me. My brother was a little bit more of a pirate and wild man than I am. I think Gerry has a certain streak of that in his makeup. On the other hand, Gerry and I have somewhat similar senses of humor and tend to see the world in the same way, so it balances.

I think perhaps the whole improvement in relationships between men and women, which I would arbitrarily date back to the emergence of the Beatles in the early sixties, has contributed to the change in fathers—the whole hippie, flower-child renovation of feeling about oneself, feeling about women, feeling about men, suddenly broke down the accepted patterns of behavior of men and women with each other. There was suddenly a much greater feeling of equality, of sharing of experiences, of life. Critics would call it blurring of roles, but I think it's a healthy development to the extent that traditional roles had unhealthy emotional patterns built into them. Men and women finally began to see each other as people. There are some historical factors at work. Perhaps the Second World War began to break down the economic stereotypes a little bit. Women had to go to work doing jobs that had been done primarily by men before they all went away to fight. I think the big increase in the wealth of the general population helped make the change possible—in other words, the traditional roles were supported to a large extent by economic necessity; when the economic necessity began to dissolve, the roles also began to change. I think women had very definite, very strong powers in the traditional structuring of roles, but to some extent they were powers that made for bad relationships—behind every man there was a little woman, sometimes knifing him in the back, or sometimes pushing him forward. It put women in a powerful but essentially manipulative position. How can you *not* resent somebody who manipulates you? It gave women an economic interest in their husbands' professional lives. That clouds the relationship and puts the woman in a semichildlike position. Who wants to do that?

I think that part of being grown up is having the ability to define your goals, to know what you can achieve and to have a plan for achieving it—to be in that position is to leave behind the negative "Freudian" aspects of one's relationship with one's father. Some people feel competitive with a parent, they feel they have to do better than their father if they think he didn't do much in what he achieved, or if they feel inferior to their father because they look down on what *they've* been able to achieve. But I think those are essentially adolescent kinds of attitudes—I don't mean to use the term as a put-down, but they're attitudes that belong to that period of life. Ultimately one acts and judges oneself according to one's own standards.

I think that any mature male has got to have had a tender and close relationship with his father. Otherwise the world in which you live as an adult would look like a pretty forbidding place.

9

Sixty-four-year-old Brooklynite Jack Schwartz is an amiable, benign manager of a women's health club. He is married and the father of two sons and a daughter. His oldest, Jeff, an attractive, huskily built thirty-two-year-old who lives in Manhattan's Sutton Place, occasionally helps his father out on weekends.

I am the last of six children. My parents were immigrants—my father was from Rumania and my mother was from Poland—and they worked seven days a week running a restaurant in our house. My mother cooked for other immigrants who were in America without their families and who were looking for home-cooked meals. My parents were really too busy trying to make a living to rear us according to today's standards, where parents try to spend more time with their children. It was the Depression, and things got so bad at one point that my mother had to go back to Europe for a while because my father couldn't support her.

All the children had to work in the restaurant, so we were around our parents a lot until we were sixteen or seventeen. When we came home from school, we had to set the tables, and in the evening we helped my father serve. We lived in the back of the restaurant, and when we were kids we slept on chairs. We'd take them from the restaurant, line them up together, put blankets on top with pillows, and that was our bed.

Our family was very close, but I think my mother was the solid one. She had drive and determination and knew how to handle people, whereas my father was less aggressive. I was closer to her, I would say. My father was not that affectionate. Well, he might have been, but he just didn't have time to show it—too many kids, too busy. I mean, things were very, very bad in those days. Plus, he was foreign born. Kids in America were sports oriented, and he knew nothing about sports. So there wasn't much you could converse with him about.

When I had children, I was determined to spend more time with them, to be with them, although I ran into the same kind of problems, working long hours to pay the bills. I went into the service during World War II, and when I got out I went to work for my brother-in-law at a factory making hats. Then I got married and borrowed money to go into business with my three brothers. We worked seventy or eighty hours a week, so I didn't have much time to spend with my three children except during slack season when I could go home a little earlier. I guess I neglected a lot of my friends then, because they weren't as important to me as my family. I got involved with Little League and that kind of thing because my sons liked sports. In fact, they still talk about it to this day. I did it so I could be with them.

My sons are thirty-two and twenty-eight and my daughter is twenty-one. My oldest son sometimes helps out at the club on Saturdays, so we get to spend that time together. My other son lives in Columbus, Ohio, and I speak to him at least once a week, sometimes more. I think my sons would give me the highest honors. I mean, I don't like to brag about myself or anything, but I would hope they would say I was a good father to them, and that if they had a problem, I was there for them to talk to.

I think I could have done a better job, though, if I hadn't had to put in so many hours a week. Most of the time when I got home during the week, they were already sleeping. I envied my wife, for having more time with them, and yet on the other hand I felt sorry for her because all the brunt of the work fell on her. It wasn't fair, but what could I do? Money had to be brought home and bills had to be paid.

There were just so many joys to fatherhood. I used to love it on Sunday mornings when they'd all come into the bedroom and start jumping on me and horsing and kidding around, and then I'd get up and make breakfast for everyone. That was a lot of fun.

I agree 100 percent with this new trend for fathers to participate more. I think it's very important. It's marvelous for fathers to take care of babies. I got up in the middle of the night and gave my children their bottles if I knew my wife was too tired. I feel that men today should take more responsibility for their children. Too many men—and women—want to socialize too much. That seems to be all they have on their minds. Every weekend they have to be out having a good time. They've got to go somewhere and do something with friends, and so forth, and the children are just pushed off. If you bring children into this world, it's your duty to do a good job with them. Don't neglect them. You'll have all the problems later on. The more attention and affection you give them, the better people they'll be, and the better later life *you'll* have. Forget about the immediate pleasures you want to have from going out, going to this party and that party, keeping up with the latest fads. Your kids *need* you. Who's going to lead them? Who's going to tell them what to do? Are they going to have to pick it up on their own? Well, if they do, they might pick up the wrong thing. This book could be a guideline for men, to tell them that when you have children, you have responsibilities and you had better stick to them—otherwise *don't* have children. There is nothing more important than bringing a person into the world.

I can relate to Dad as a man and not just as my father: we work together, we socialize together [said Jeff Schwartz]. I see him interacting with other people and I can stand back and look at him as a human being, almost without being his son. I can look at him without being judgmental. He's the nicest man I know; I think it's pretty rare for a child to say that about a parent—at least people *I've* come across. As far as being a *father,* he is an excellent, dedicated father. In fact, he's almost *too* dedicated, too self-sacrificing. He has devoted all his time to me and to my brother and sister, but I hope that he feels it's reward enough to know we love him.

I had a great childhood. Both my parents, but my father especially, always participated with me when I was a youngster. Dad was the coach for the Little League and he was in charge of Boy Scouts. When my friends wanted to go out to the pizza place or somewhere, it was always my dad who drove everybody. He took us all over, to museums, to zoos. He really dedicated the time he had to us—and there wasn't much of it, because he worked six days a week and he came home late at night. The other fathers in the neighborhood were more aloof when it came to their children. They were more self-centered, they had less time for their children and couldn't relate to them. They didn't want to be part of their children's lives and they left it all up to their wives. My father didn't. He took an interest in us: we were the most important things in his life.

My mother was always the disciplinarian. Actually there was a *lack* of discipline from my father. This is not necessarily a reversal of roles. It was a Jewish household, and if you want to view it ethnically, the mother is usually the domineering one. I became something of a rebel because of that. As a child, looking at my father, loving him so much, I would think, Why is my father letting my mother dominate him and push him around? I've adopted this in my personality: I don't allow women to push me around.

My father and I were very physically affectionate. To this day I still kiss him. I'll do it after a long absence, or if something has made me happy, or I'll just look at him and say, "Hey, I love you,

Dad. Come here." And I'll give him a hug without any feeling of embarrassment. I am aware that this is not the norm, but I believe that women *and* men should show affection. There is nothing wrong with a man showing affection, not at all. As a matter of fact, it's healthy. I was just talking to a man on the telephone the other day. He happens to be fairly young, forty-four years old. He had just come out of major surgery, and when he got home he started crying. He was crying with joy just to be home, to have his family around, because he had been so near death. Anyway, he called me and said, "Jeff, I think there's something wrong with me. I'm feeling strange. I'm feeling euphoric. I cried to my daughter and I cried to my son. I *never* cry." And I told him, "Ivan, there's nothing wrong with crying. You're showing emotion. You don't have to be this hard Rock of Gibraltar that television and movies and propaganda have made you into." He said, "I know, I know. I'm a product of my environment. But I'm working on it."

I'd say compared with my male peers, I'm more the exception than the rule. They're more macho. Macho is the best description I can give. They're all on ego trips, they have a lot of hang-ups, they're not comfortable with themselves, they're always trying to impress other people. They lack self-evaluation.

If my father had been aloof and unaffectionate, I'd most definitely be different today. Probably one of the reasons I've always examined myself is because my father gave me warmth and kindness. He let me develop in my own way, which made me sensitive to my surroundings and to my self. I'm not saying I never had problems. Of course I did. But my father's warmth and kindness helped: it gave me the freedom to look at things and it gave me the open-mindedness to examine myself.

My relationship with Dad has always been close; the love has always been consistent. When I *didn't* get along with him, it was usually because of other family interactions. A lot of it had to do with my mother. I felt he was not quite strong enough with her. He was too kind, which I interpreted in my teen years as a weakness rather than a strength. But I didn't realize back then why I was angry at the whole situation. It hurt during those years knowing he thought of me as a troublemaker. But I always knew he loved me. No matter what I did, there was always love. He would say, "Oh, God, you did it again," but there was a reinforcement of love at the same time. He never made me feel rotten or rejected. He knows I'm his son, and he knows I'm basically like him. I am very much like my dad—I've *tried* to be very much like him. In business I've been taken advantage of because I've been too easy and trusting. There's a hard-core world out there, and you get stepped on when you're like that. But I'm idealistic, and I refuse to give up those values. They are excellent qualities.

I will absolutely have children. I love children. My father was such a good father that I would try to be the father he's been to me. In most ways. I would be more in touch with what my wife was doing with the children. The woman I marry will have to be a special woman, very much dedicated to having children.

I think this Oedipal theory is a bunch of bull, myself. Family situations can *create* problems; the interaction between a husband and wife and the rivalry between members of a family can create hostilities, but I don't think they're instinctively in us. Tenderness and affection is as characteristic of a father-son relationship as this so-called conflict is: I mean, monkeys are tender and affectionate. And does the little boy monkey really hate his father and lust after his mother? I don't know the answer to that, but I seriously doubt it.

My father was as much a nurturer as my mother. We didn't see him as often, but on Saturdays he used to take me in to the factory with him and I got to work there. It made me feel fantastic. There was a camaraderie, we had something in common: *Hey, I'm with my dad.*

As I've gotten older, I guess I've realized that things are not so cut and dried. People are human and they have frailties. There are all kinds of extenuating circumstances. I can relate more to my father as a friend now. We do a lot together, we go to Knicks games, we go on fishing trips every summer, we go to the fights, to Madison Square Garden. Now, I'm not that crazy about these things, except fishing. But I know he gets such pleasure out of it. He wants to be with me.

I just hope I strike it rich before I have children, because I'd like to spend every day with them. I won't have a child unless I'm going to dedicate my life to him. It's one of the biggest responsibilities that anyone can have, to bring another human being into the world. You are responsible for helping that person become a self-sufficient individual with the right morals, the right values—someone who will be prepared for life. I plan on my wife having natural childbirth, and I'll be there when my child is born. I'll deliver it. I'll be part of his life from the start.

10

Born in Eastern Europe and now an American citizen, Ahmet Temel* is a Ph.D. candidate in engineering. His father, a judge, died several years ago. Mr. Temel is married to an American designer. They have no children.

I was working in a fertilizer plant on the coast of the Black Sea one summer in my second year of college, and my father came to visit. He was with Mother and the kids on vacation in a summer house in Ankara and he came over to visit me. I was feeling more grown up then and we spent that time like friends rather than as father and son. They were memorable days. I was very happy during that time. It was just the two of us together, going to places we'd never seen before.

It is a very delicate thing, being a father and friend. You depend on your father when you're a kid. He shows you everything, you know. And when he visited me, I was showing him around because he didn't know anything about engineering. I was teaching him, actually. We were equals at that level. And when we were taking tours, it was the same way; we were enjoying it at the same level. He wasn't showing me something that he had seen before.

He was the strict-in-principles type of father. He set some

disciplinary rules and I would never disagree. But that was pretty good, because otherwise I wouldn't have a strong personality, I guess. It helped me to develop my own principles, in a way, because he was the example. I could never smoke a cigarette in front of him, or drink alcohol except for a beer—that wasn't allowed. It was partly tradition, although I'd seen other people do it outside our family.

There was a great deal of affection in our family. We used to just sit together, and he would kiss me, all my sisters, the same way— kissing, hugging, calling us by dear names, lovely names. He would do it under any circumstances. We might just walk up to each other and kiss or hug. If we went away on a trip, when we got back there would always be this glorious type of affection.

He wasn't that flexible—that's one thing I would have changed about him. In setting certain rules of discipline, he was a very conservative, strict father. I was twenty when he died, and I don't know what I would have thought had he lived until I was twenty-four or twenty-five.

His death surprised all of us. But in a sense it helped me to develop my personality. I had to assume all the responsibility for my family, I had to learn about life. There are certain things I am strong at, and I guess I have the leader's character.

The best thing he taught me was to speak the truth. He never lied, except for childhood things like Santa Claus. He was a truthful and strong person, a determined person. He was in politics, but I'm more a politician than he was, in every way. What I mean by being a politician is that you should have flexibility. You should know how to handle the situation either by smiling at people or hugging them or saying, "Oh you're a great person." He was a very judgmental person, and if something was wrong, he'd say, "Wrong!" I'm not like that. I'll look at the results first.

My father wanted me to be either a lawyer or an engineer. He believed in my intelligence, and I proved him right. As in all father-son relationships, my style was different, my expectations were different—but that didn't really affect the existence of love between us.

I remember once he slapped me, and it really hurt and I ran into my room and started crying. After a while he came in and there were tears in his eyes and he hugged me and kissed me. I was very pleased about that. I remember that very well.

When he died, I thought that I loved my father more than I loved my mother: I don't know why. It's an unexplainable thing. It could be a bond between father and son. I loved my father's personality, always being on the side of truth. I also liked the respect he had from other people; I wanted to be like him.

Oh, yes, he praised us, but it was a very measured praise; he never spoiled us. For example, I was never given a *gift* for my accomplishments.

Males are dominant in the old country, and yet affection exists among them. You see it as much between fathers and sons as between mothers and daughters. After a certain age sons want to act and be like their fathers. They like to live in the same house up until the time they get married.

My father was actually not as friendly with me as I would have liked. That's a very important point. I always wanted to go and talk to him about my cigarette smoking, for example, and drinking alcohol and I never could. Anyway I wouldn't take these things so seriously if I had a son: If he wants to smoke he can. I would tell him that it's dangerous, and I would try to stop him if it is in my power. I think there should be a balance: spank a son when it is necessary, kiss him when it is necessary. There should be that kind of measure.

I would probably rather have a son than a daughter, mainly to lead our family. But that's the only reason actually. And I think he would be closer to me than a girl: I could take him places with me, like to hunt or to ride horses.

It's very important to spend time with a child. I feel my father spent enough time with me. When I was growing up he and I would take long walks together. He would take me to his office once in a while. I would play around and sometimes bother him. He was in the courtroom once, and right in the middle of a case I walked in; he had to call the doorman to take me out. I didn't like his office, but it was a very fine feeling to be there. We were always together, actually. I didn't have trouble seeing him until I started college. I felt at that time that we were starting a new phase of the relationship. I was going out at night and coming home after he was asleep.

I didn't cry at his death; I felt I had to be strong, to take care of things. Then after some time I cried. It's a good feeling to have a father: he's not like anybody else. I still always feel the grief that I don't have him.

I think the first word that comes to mind when I hear father-son relationship is love.

11

George Callimanis* is a thirty-year-old bachelor who grew up in the Greek community of Astoria, Queens. Mr. Callimanis worked as bartender for his father, a onetime nightclub owner, before becoming a hairstylist in Manhattan.

My father and I get along very well; in fact, he gave me a great deal of inspiration in business. He owned a couple of nightclubs, and I used to work for him as a bartender.

He would always let me be me although he taught me and advised me. My father made sure we always looked good and dressed nice and he was affectionate with the whole family. At night he used to come into our rooms and kiss us—I have two other brothers. I'm the oldest. We're all a happy family.

In the beginning I was closer to my mother because she was always around. I didn't see my father a lot: he was always so busy. Now it's equal—I'm close to both of them. My father's retired now, and whatever chance I get, I go visit them at home in Astoria. My parents were born in Greece, and Astoria is a Greek community. My father was always interested in what we were doing; he made sure we kept up with the Greek religion; we're actually like a European family would be. He really cared about our activities.

My father was a man who always told our mother never to hit us; he didn't like the idea of hitting his children. He never raised a hand to any of us. That's why I guess we were always a happy family.

He never put pressure on us to succeed and we could do anything we wished to do. I've had quite a few occupations. When I was working on cars, my father was always with me, you know. He never said not to do something. He directed us, and offered to help us out. When I started doing hair, my father was my mannequin; he'd let me give him three-hour haircuts. He never raised objections to the hair business.

He was always on my side. I remember one time I was working in a food store, and he drove by with my mother. I had carried about fifty-two watermelons that day, and later my mother told me that my father couldn't stand watching me do all this. I guess he really felt for me. That was my first and last day.

I think the best thing about my father is that he was always there. It is always nice and secure to know that your father and mother are there, to have them ask you how everything is. Even today.

I really have nothing bad to say about my father. I guess it would have been nice to have him around more in the beginning, to have him come to things when we were in high school, and so on. My mother was the one who came.

I think my father's very proud of me. No matter what I did, no matter what career, I tried to be tip-top.

I think it's important to have communication between father and son at all times. Even if it's something that the father hates to hear about. There should be love.

12

He is a tennis buff with a solidly athletic build and the kind of restless energy that has made it possible for him to successfully juggle several careers at once. Currently Steve Conn, a forty-two-year-old bachelor, works as a journalist and a cable TV consultant. His love of the outdoors is so die-hard, he makes his official at-home office in the garden of his Upper East Side Manhattan apartment. The following interview took place in the garden, purely by coincidence on the anniversary of the death of his mother, the event which, he says, was most responsible for bringing him closer to his father.

My dad worked long hours in service stations and he never really liked the work. He'd leave about seven in the morning, just as I was going off to school, and he wouldn't get back until around seven at night, and by then I'd be doing my homework. We were lucky if we had dinner together, and then that was that. I didn't see much of him except on weekends. I was very close to my mother. After she died in 1959, just before my twenty-first birthday, I became tremendously close to my father because essentially all he had was me and all I had was him.

When I was growing up I would discuss everything with my mother. She was a great woman, the driving force in the family. My father is a great man but I think the Depression took a terrific toll on him. He was a product of the Depression. He and his father worked together in the fish business and they were completely wiped out by the Depression. This had a tremendous impact on my dad. It made him incredibly conservative and cautious—incredibly!

If he could just bring enough home so that his family got along, that to him was security. Here was a man who could have done great things, who could have had a fine profession and contributed to society. But because he'd been hurt so badly in the Depression he never became a fighter or took the chances that are necessary for real success in this world. I think I became a fighter—and I really am a fighter, I'm not afraid of *anything*—as a reaction to my father's introversion and how it held him back professionally. I, too, was very conservative until I went into the army, though. I was in intelligence doing very dangerous, James Bond stuff, and that experience has made me fiercely independent. Dad lives a lot of his life through me—not only through the stories I write, but also through my many battles for the poor and disadvantaged in the course of my extensive public service work.

But anyway, I was so close to my mother that any decision that had to be made I discussed with her, not with Dad. He was too busy working all the time and I didn't see that much of him. When I was with him, however, we were doing very happy, positive things together. We went to Brooklyn Dodger baseball games at Ebbets Field; we played ball together, and those things meant a lot to me when I was a kid. My dad was there on weekends and he was always there to do things I wanted to do. We were both outstanding athletes and the basis of our relationship then was sports. My dad had one wish in the world. You know what that was? He wanted me to become the lightweight boxing champion of the world. Not a doctor, a great journalist, a public servant or anything like that. When I was four years old, he gave me a pair of boxing gloves as a birthday present. He put them on me and boxed with me. Well, I was never a good boxer, but my father wanted me to become a boxer. Why? Because when he was a kid, he was a top-flight amateur boxer. He worked out at Stillman's gym, where Joe Louis and all the greats worked and hung out. He was taken under the wing of Benny Leonard, the lightweight champion of the world. My father *worshipped* Benny Leonard. He wanted to become lightweight champ himself, but he got into other things. He had to work for a living. So his wish became for *me,* or my older brother, to become champion. You know how a lot of fathers are with sons—they want to see them do the things *they* really wanted to do. But I made the choice early on that I didn't want to pursue athletics as a career even though I was an excellent all-round athlete. I was the most valuable player on the Brooklyn Championship softball team; I was on the Erasmus Hall High School track team, I did *everything.* But I wanted to live a full life—the kind of life I have now.

My dad is introverted and shy and even now that makes some things difficult. He's eighty years old and I would like him to go out and join senior citizens' groups where they have discussions and various activities, but he refuses. So I end up going back and forth from Manhattan to Brooklyn, not only to keep him company but also to take care of the house. He won't even let me bring a woman in on a regular basis to clean or cook. He's an incredibly private individual and I think he sees an outsider coming in as an intrusion on his privacy. As soon as I lost my mother I knew I was going to have to spend more time with Dad. When I got out of graduate school and the service, I made him quit his job because I didn't like the kind of work he was doing. So I have supported my father since 1961. We had a tremendous fight over that. My dad has a terrific amount of pride. He didn't want to stop working. He always wanted to take care of himself. But I said, "Look, Dad, I'm working and making money now and some of this money is going to go to you. You helped send me to college and grad school. You and Mother did an awful lot for me, and I've got to repay you." I know you don't just help people you love with money; you give them other things, too, which are important. But I wanted to take care of my father. So I made him quit his job and he did— reluctantly—because he loves me.

I travel an awful lot and I've taken Dad with me many times. I love the Caribbean and I've taken him along with me and my girl friends. The three of us would do things together during the day. He was a great swimmer and loved the beach and we'd spend time on the beach and then I'd take them both to dinner in the evenings. Part of the purpose of taking Dad was to expose him to the better things in life. The only rebelliousness I ever had against my father was a rebellion against his tremendous conservatism because I saw how he never really wanted much in the material sense. I've always wanted to live a good life, and I've always wanted a good life for those near and dear to me. Dad lives with his two dogs on the barest essentials in his apartment in Flatbush, but that's the way he wants it. I went back to Brooklyn to take care of Dad when he was ill a few years ago, and the six months of living with him in the old apartment where I grew up was extremely depressing. Thomas Wolfe is right—you can't go home again. Now I speak with Dad by phone several times each day and I go back a couple of days each week to be with him and see to his needs. With my peripatetic schedule it can get tough at times. I vowed many years ago never to put my father in a nursing home, and I never will. Every winter, when he was still able to travel, I'd take him down to Florida or out to the West Coast to get him out of the cold weather, and because I wanted to facilitate a transition from the old neighborhood. I wanted to eventually buy him a condominium in Florida. But when push came to shove he told me it would make him terribly depressed to live down there. And then I understood that he's got his roots in Flatbush and he'll never leave it. I knew I'd finally lost the battle when he told me one day, "Steve, I want to die in this apartment." And all the money I've given him for twenty years— and believe me, I had to fight to make him take it—you know what he did? He's lived so abstemiously—you wouldn't believe it, he didn't spend a cent—he put every penny in the bank so it would eventually go back to me. Now I've got all this money in trust and I've invested it for both of us. But I still give him money every month, as always.

My father had only three weeks of a high school education, but he's extremely well read and articulate and very bright. His views on current events and politics are very cogent and informed. If he'd pursued his education further he could have become extremely successful and devoted himself to doing good things. He has amazing integrity. Both my parents were good, honest, hard-working people. They would never, under any circumstances, steal, lie or cheat, and I think that gave me a strong sense of moral values, and also of the need to serve people. My father is basically a simple man, but he has a lot of class. He is a great man—a great class man.

13

Benjamin MacKay,* employed as a computer analyst in the South, is a sociology graduate with a highly astute, ruminative turn of mind. In his darkened garden apartment, still stacked with boxes and scattered with papers from his recent move, he remembered his late father, a public relations executive. Mr. MacKay is single and in his thirties.

My father was a very interesting, intelligent, well-read man. He was hard for me to deal with when I was younger, because he was always ten feet above my head. Not only physically but mentally, and that was reinforced by everyone I ever met. They'd say, "Oh, you're Benjamin MacKay's son." I was Benjamin, Jr., but when I went to college I was Ben because we traveled in the same circles. So I became Ben instead of Benjamin to be differentiated—not to be just Benjamin MacKay's son.

It's very difficult when you start out as a child with a parent you're always looking up to, and then every corner you turn there's someone saying, "You're Benjamin MacKay's son, he's a very intelligent man, he did this, this, this and this." You tend to grow up in opposition, which is very limiting. Anything he ever did, I'd do the opposite. He wrote and I would never write, although I have a talent for it. He played bridge; I played chess. I admired him, of course—it's hard not to admire someone about whom you're constantly being told—and would have liked, probably, to have been like him. But I did resent it, being just his son. And as I said, I grew up in opposition to his personality because I wanted to be my own person. I'm the second oldest child and the oldest son—there are five sons and two daughters. Because I was the oldest, I had the most pressure to perform.

It's tough going through adolescence trying to resolve those feelings. But I was fortunate enough when I went to college to finally sit down and talk to my father as a person, rather than someone I looked up to. Even though I had been bigger than him for a number of years, I still had the carry-over from childhood—that he was so far over my head physically. Basically he was very meek. It was a revelation to talk to him and realize, My God, he's a human being.

We got to a stage where it wasn't a father-son relationship. We just became friends. I was fortunate to get to know him in that respect—to find out he had weaknesses, too, so I could put aside all those years of resentment when I was under his thumb.

A lot of my feeling was due to my mother saying "Your father's so brilliant, your father's so brilliant." I was in a no-win situation. Personally, when it gets right down to it, I think my mother's motive was to make me dependent on her because my father wasn't home a lot when I was growing up. He ran a public relations firm so it meant a lot of outside entertaining. He was at his club every day for lunch with clients and he stayed out late and didn't come home a lot, so we saw very little of him when I was growing up. When he did come home, we were so much in awe of him that we really could not relate. Which is sad, because we were afraid to ask him for anything. And yet he was the one person who would give it to us if we *did* ask. A lot of this was not his fault, it was my own perspective. As I told you, when I got to college and could sit and talk to him eye to eye, I got to know him as a fallible person, someone who was real. That's when I was older and could look and see that some of the things going on that might have slighted me weren't his fault. He had no control over them because he *was* a human being and not the omnipotent person I perceived him to be.

We were close growing up to the extent that he would sit for hours playing chess with me, and he'd go throw the football with me and things like that, on weekends. Most of the time, though, he was out hustling. When you have eight people to support, you have to spend a lot of time out hustling, especially if you have your own company. We really didn't talk when we played chess. It was "This is what you do, you do it this way, or that way," rather than "What do you think you should do?" He was the instructor, the authority figure, and that was one of the problems. When I finally beat him at chess, I never played again. It felt *great.* And he was *mad.* He was very upset. On the other hand, he would praise me for my accomplishments, like when I did well in school.

My father did spend a lot of time with my older sister and me when we were much younger. There's a big gap in our family—my sister and me, and then five years later the next child. Then as the family grew he had to spend more time at work. When we moved to Oklahoma, he worked in the public relations department of a college. He was very involved in campus life and knew a lot of people. He was always with the people who were *happening.* He liked to be with stimulating people, with politicians, with moneyed people. He liked to argue philosophy and economics, even though he was self-taught in a lot of things. When he died he had basically solved all his emotional problems. He'd finally gotten a handle on everything. After trying to work out his relationship with my mother, he found they were two incompatible people. He was a socialite and she was a stay-at-home type. He even got a maid so my mother could go downtown and entertain with him, but she would stay home and talk to *me.*

His death affected me dramatically. When he died, I was the first told. My best friend came to my apartment and knocked on my door at four o'clock in the morning and told me that my father was dead. It was a very difficult time for me because I didn't have a moment to breathe. I had to handle all the arrangements—the insurance, the death certificate, the funeral. Probably two years later, I cried. When he died I shut it out completely. I just built a wall against it. Because I built a wall, I didn't really grieve. I was in a state of nonfeeling. I felt guilty about that, and finally I was able to cry and I was able to talk about it. The worst thing for me after he died was missing him on campus. The last year of school I'd see someone coming around the corner who had a bald head like him and suddenly it would hit me: "God, my father's *dead.* I'll never see him coming around the corner anymore." And when your father dies, you immediately know you're mortal.

I think of all the things that did not get said, or said enough—specifically, "I really do love you, I care about you." A month or two before he died, we'd been to the local college bar, and we talked, and told each other, "I love you, I really do love you." He talked to me about his problems with my mother, and I could *see* them. We talked about working together. It probably could have happened, he and I running the business. All that went down the drain. I was lucky enough, more than my brothers and sisters, to get to know him as a person. Love and tenderness characterized our relationship much more than hostility and resentment toward the end.

I'll tell you how he'd probably describe me as a son—very admiring. Anything I became interested in, he was interested in. But it took me until I was twenty years old to recognize that. The people I liked in college, he became fast friends with. The professors I liked in the English department he would go out of his way to have drinks with, to find out what I was doing, where I was going, because I couldn't tell him. I was a freshman, a sophomore in college, experiencing freedom. I thought he was interfering, and yet he was going out of his way *not* to interfere.

My father wasn't stern enough, if you want to know the truth—he didn't sit me down and weigh on my tail when it was necessary. When a child is punished for something, it shouldn't just be, "I'll take your bike away for three months," and then you're on it again the next day. This is ridiculous. I think physical punishment is necessary. When we're children we're not little adults. We definitely need the slap on the butt. If you don't get it you resent it in a way, because you don't feel your parent cares. Luckily, I found out he really did care, but my brothers never did. It has affected them detrimentally. They don't know what he was except through my mother's eyes which are slightly jaundiced. Now they're fumbling around, trying to be men. If he'd died when I was twelve or sixteen, I don't think I could have handled it either. I know from talking to my brothers and sisters that *they* can't. The person they perceive is so different from the real man.

I believe the most important thing a father can give a son is his love—expressed in a real sense, not just saying "Hey, I love you," and letting it go at that. The most important thing in *our* relationship were those talks we had toward the end—after I got to know him and we had shed a few tears and had dropped all our defenses and our retention of emotions and could look eye to eye, man to man, and say, I love you.

If my father were alive today, our relationship would be much closer than when I was growing up. I especially miss him now that I'm going through a lot of changes in my life. I'd like to be able to talk to him. He could subjectively-objectively look at a situation because he had been through a lot of things in his life. Your father is the one you can really talk to. He would be the only person in your life besides your mother who is totally for *you*. You can say, "What the hell should I do?" Whether you take the advice or not, you know you're going to get an honest answer. I miss that terribly.

If I could change anything about our relationship, it would be that I wouldn't have slighted him the way I did. When he reached out, I moved back.

A few months before his death I went to a lot of parties with him. He was dating a woman who was in the higher strata of society and he pulled me along to meet the people who were very interesting to him. But I kinda rejected it at the time. I was more interested in being a fraternity boy.

If I have children, I'd probably rather have daughters. This is a male's viewpoint, of course, but I think girls are a little bit easier to handle than boys. Fathers can be more emotional with daughters, simply because they're girls. It's not socially acceptable to be emotional with sons. The society we're in now, it's hard for a man to just say to a son, "I love you." It's a cultural lag and maybe things will be better in the next generation because there's been so much research and people are more aware. *I'm* more aware. If I had a son, I'd touch him and hug him and kiss him. As in any relationship, you can't *not* touch. For me it breaks a barrier down. If I touch you and you withdraw, it makes me feel awful. The night we talked in that bar, the barrier fell down, and we cried and hugged. I let him into me and he let me into him. It's kind of a cliché to say it, but it was a celebration. We were one. We were happy and sad and everything was all right.

14

The traditional tale of following in father's footsteps in business was given something of a twist when Colin Grant, thirty-nine, preceded his father in a brokerage house in New England. The younger Mr. Grant had been an officer in the company for several years when Winthrop Grant took over as chairman last year after a career as a banker.

My father was a very strong, domineering sort of man [says Winthrop Grant]. He had no formal schooling, but he was an exceedingly educated man. He read constantly and he had a very inquiring, interested mind. He was a great teacher and I remember literally thousands of things that he told me of his own experiences, and things that were of great help to me later on. I was extremely fond of him. I didn't really spend that much time with him, but the time I did spend seemed to count. We weren't buddies; that wasn't our relationship. We didn't go camping together or that sort of thing. It was more of a teacher-student sort of relationship. But at least I had sense enough to listen.

He had tremendous influence in my life. I think he guided me well. I spent my life the wrong way, but that has nothing to do with it. I never wanted to live in New England after the war. I wanted to go away, to the Bay area of California. I'm glad now I didn't, but at the time I really wound up doing what he wanted me to do. He was a merchant, but he didn't want me to go into his business because it wasn't one he wanted to keep. He never encouraged me to do that, and so I think the next best thing, the easiest thing, was for me to go into finance. Which I did. I was president of a small bank for many years, until I took over as chairman of this brokerage house where my son was already working.

I have two sons. In Colin's case I went through a period with him that got a little hairy; it wasn't long, but he revolted—I guess when he was fifteen or sixteen. I never really knew what he was revolting *against*. He would disobey me—generally things that didn't require corporal punishment—but I never did figure out why. It was just a revolt, period, I think. I remember one time I was at our summer house in Maine. Colin was working there and I came out one weekend and found the whole wall of the porch full of holes. He'd stood there and thrown an ice pick at it. That was the kind of thing he would do.

Colin got to know his grandfather well. All the grandchildren would go over to his house on Sunday afternoons, and he'd have tents in the yard, and music and all sorts of things. He'd deliver them back after supper, and that went on for years. Well, of course, the grandchildren got to know each other and got to know him and so they had that relationship. He didn't ooh and aah and pick them up and do things like that, but he did all the mental gymnastics with them. That's what he liked. It was not physical affection at all; that's the way he was with me, too.

I never felt deprived. Somehow my father satisfied me. Maybe because I was the same way, I don't know. He never left any doubt that he had affection or love for me. I knew it because he was always trying to anticipate what was coming up for me. We never stayed out of contact long. When I was at West Point we'd write with regularity, and during the war he always wrote to me. And if someone important was in town and came out to the house, I'd be included. It's really kind of hard to describe, but I always felt an affection from him.

I'm afraid I was the same with my sons, except that I don't think I was the teacher that my father was. I think that maybe I failed in that respect. I didn't go camping and all that stuff with the boys, but we did have a summer house in the woods, and during the summer they'd move up there. I'd come out on weekends, so we rode horseback and had time together. I tried to be fair with them, and I tried to teach them a little something about honesty and things like that.

I think that Colin has realized the importance of his children, of the boys not becoming mama's boys, and I think he's making a conscious effort to be with them a lot. I know he's taken the older one camping. I've never talked to him about it, but I think he has done more of that than I did.

Today fathers do participate more in their children's lives. There's this joint birth thing now, but I think I would have *fainted* being in the delivery room. The concept is great though; I'm all for it, I think it's just fine.

I'm a little vague, I guess, in lots of ways, and I'm not affectionate in the sense of showing affection—at least my wife always tells me that. My mother's side of the family was very stoic, very quiet people. I think maybe I've inherited some of those traits. I've always had a lot of Jewish friends; I like Jewish people because they're almost *overly* emotional with their families. I've got a wartime friend, and we visit in Rhode Island, and he is very outwardly emotional with his wife. During the war he was always talking about Martha, and Martha's picture was always around, and I admired that. It was not my way, but I admired it, I liked it. It's the old school; that's the way they were raised, with this great show of affection. They have a strong sense of family.

I don't know whether I *could* change anything. I'm not a good actor, you might say. I always sort of got by with "I am what I am," and that may not be enough. My father used to say, "Look your best, son, because your best is none too good."

What makes a good father? Caring. I at least did this: the kids knew I wanted to know what they were doing and where they were and who they were with, and I sometimes didn't hesitate if their associates were not good to discourage those relationships. That was my style, which was different from my father's, but maybe to some degree it accomplished the same thing.

I think raising kids is a hairy proposition, and some of the nicest people I know have some of the worst problems. It's hard for me to understand. We've got some friends who are just fine people, and they have three of the worst kids—dope and every sort of problem. I just can't imagine it. But I think there is something to the idea that you have to be *around*.

We traveled a lot with our kids when they were young, and I remember one time my wife said, "Let's you and I go for a long trip." And I said, "Why now?" And she said, "Well, the cat's going to have kittens and Colin's going to get his driver's license, and that'll be the end." So some baby-sitters stayed with the boys. But generally we took them along.

I don't like working as closely as I do with my son. That was my real concern about taking the position with the brokerage house, and that's one reason I want to ease out when I can. I think it's been a horrible handicap to him. He was here before I came, and there's a rule in this company that family members can't work together. Nobody ever said anything about it; everybody just closed their eyes. But it's not good. I think everybody's bending over backwards—*I'm* bending over backwards—to be sure he doesn't get an advantage because of his relationship with me. If I owned the company and was going to pass it on to him, it'd be different; what the hell, who'd care? As it is, it's a handicap.

I didn't want him to transfer. Originally I wanted him to go to New York to start out, and he dutifully went there and went through the motions and tried, but he came back.

My Father, My Son

My relationship with my father has been very good in the last few years [said Colin Grant]. I had some really stormy times with him when I was in high school, maybe even as early as junior high school. I didn't want to go to Viet Nam, and he's a flag waver and he raised hell with me about that. My father has always been a fair man and a good man, but he's been a negative reinforcer. He never in my life told me I did anything good: if the grade was a *D* and it should have been a *B,* instead of picking out something good to reinforce, he'd just clobber me on the head and say, "You're never going to get to college, you're never going to do anything," and that kind of stuff.

Dad wasn't a terribly ambitious man in the sense of trying to make as much money as possible; money has never been a goal in his life, which is good. But he was interested in his career and it took away a lot of the time he might have spent with my brother and me pitching softball or something like that. He'd come home in the evenings, but it was hard to sit down and have a conversation with him. He had a huge stack of material to read; he was a compulsive reader.

Now, things are good, but back then he was hard for me to talk to; I always felt a little bit inferior to him. My brother *really* felt it—it's bothered him more than me. We both felt somewhat inferior to Dad because he was very successful and much more educated than we were. My father and my father's father were tremendously respected in town, and it's hard to fill those shoes.

I really needed support from my father, but I didn't know how to ask for it and he didn't know how to give it. He probably isn't even aware of it *today.* But he was fair, too, at the same time. If he was coming down on me all the time it was because he wanted me to do well. He wanted good things for my brother and me. But it was kind of tough to handle. When I say I rebelled, I didn't drop out of school and out of sight. I am basically conservative, and when I go off center of that it's only about five degrees.

127

I've always been someone who never quite knew what he wanted to do; I got out of high school and had not really prepared myself for any career pursuits. I didn't know what I wanted to study, where I wanted to go to college. A friend of mine was going to a school in Vermont so I decided to go there too. I got in by the skin of my teeth. After two years I went to the University of Massachusetts. At the end of my junior year I made a substantial change in my life; I got married and changed my degree major from liberal arts to business.

When I got out of college Dad didn't want me to come to this firm. You see, my grandfather was president and chairman of the board at the time. A Grant has been in this firm since the mid- to late sixties, either as a director of chief executive officer or something. Again, it was a case of negative reinforcement. It wasn't that he didn't want me there: He was trying to keep me out of a bad situation. And it *has* been hard for me. Hell, half the employees here when I started had worked under my grandfather. And they thought, Well, you know this guy can't get favored treatment!

I've had to work doubly hard to get to the same position as anybody else—from my viewpoint, anyway. It's been highly frustrating at times. I know in the last two or three years I've brought in a great deal of business, and yet not quite enough to be a vice president. Anyway, I did weasel my way into the firm against Dad's wishes and I've lived through a lot of the stuff that he was trying to protect me from. But instead of his really explaining it, we had some bitterness when I got out of college because he said, "Get out of here; you need to get out of town and go to New York and make some money and make a name for yourself *there.*"

When the board brought my dad in as chairman last year I thought, boy, this is it. The fact that we had clashed at times didn't help, but he made a deal with the board going in. He wanted to remove himself as much as possible from any authority over me, and he's let that be widely known. He is a good, fair man,

128

and the other officers in the company quickly recognized that there wasn't going to be any collusion between the two of us, and it's really worked great. I think he's seen that I have made some strides in establishing my own name, and since that time we have really gotten to be close. He recognizes me as someone who's kind of made it, and I think he's proud of me.

Dad's really reserved. He's not an openly loving person; he never hugged me or anything but I knew he cared about me. You just know it. But I think I would have wanted more demonstrative affection.

I'm not sure I ever understood my dad, but I knew he was a basically great person. Everybody looked up to him, and I felt like I needed to stay around to find out why. He's great in a lot of ways; I've never met anybody as fair in business and personal life; he's never compromised his morals one minute. That's why he's not in public service anymore.

I also respect his intelligence; he's a very well-read man. I hated to read, and I think it goes back to my grandfather. We used to go to his house on Sunday afternoons, and he would sit down with me and—gosh, I must have been about six or seven—he'd throw Robert Louis Stevenson at me and say, "You read this." It was a monumental task; consequently, I never read for pleasure.

I'm extremely loving with my oldest son, Parker, who's six. The youngest is only nine months, and at that stage all you can do is sort of hold them and sling them around in your arms while they pull your glasses off. I have very consciously spent time with the oldest one. I think a father has got to have a commitment. Caring is one thing—I mean, my father cared more about us than anything in the world, but he cared from afar. What matters is to be there on a daily basis.

I never was involved in sports, so I've tried to get my son involved in them, which he really has not wanted to do. He doesn't seem to be able to take much pressure. Soccer came along this year and he decided he didn't want to do it, and I decided I'm not going to pressure him at all. I just say, "I think soccer's really a good sport" and let it go at that. At any rate, I've gotta be careful about suggesting certain things to him. Maybe I've put pressures on him in the past, although I'm not aware of them, but I damn sure don't want to put pressure on him now. Gosh, I hope I never put any negative reinforcement on him like my father did on me.

Last year we entered him in a little swim meet at the country club, and he came home with a lot of the ribbons. And then we got this thing going, "Well, Dad, *you* never win any ribbons—I win them all." And he nails them up on his door, and he comes in to see me and says, "Well, when are *you* gonna win one?" But I think he's getting involved because of peer pressure now. Parker's really interested in museums and reading and things like that. That's his world and I think he's going to get somewhere. He goes to a private school and I've occasionally gone out there and showed up for lunch. Man, he just loves it.

The sixties changed a lot of things; there was so much turmoil then. The Viet Nam war was a big deal in our family because with my father tradition and fighting for your country were such a big thing. I remember he used to come home at five o'clock every day, and we'd all sit down and watch Walter Cronkite and then eat dinner—the same thing every day.

From my viewpoint it was a frustrating deal. I didn't understand all the ramifications and the politics of the Viet Nam war. It just seemed to be a war you couldn't grab on to. I had a heart problem—nothing serious, it never bothered me—and I casually mentioned one day that I was going to use that to stay out of the draft and whew! Boy, my dad went through the roof and said, "You sure as hell aren't. You're going to fight for your country and when you're called to serve, you're going to serve." We went round and round about that. He didn't have the capacity to examine another point of view; duty calls, duty serves. He's lived his whole life that way—duty to the bank, duty to the family, duty to whatever, you know.

I wish I had had guts enough at a young age to sit down and tell Dad what I really needed, to sit down with him man to man. That's one thing I think I would change. As I said, there was a certain fear, a reverence for this giant guy. Thinking ahead, I just didn't see any way I could fill those shoes. So I didn't do *anything*. It was nothing *he* did—he wasn't pounding me over the head with it because he is very modest about anything he's ever done.

At one point I wanted to go into banking, but I didn't because he told me I didn't have any business doing that. More negative reinforcement. I think it is excellent preparation for any kind of business career; but Dad said, "Well, banking is a crappy profession. I'm lucky to have my position. There's too damn many bankers around and you can't make it without being greedy. It's a political game and you've got to run over everybody else." Basically I think he liked the theoretical aspect of economics; he didn't really care for the profession.

I've got to admit I'm very conscious of this reserved attitude I have toward my father, this fear of his stature and demeanor. But I think I've finally overcome the pitfalls of it.

15

The sun beat down relentlessly on the 2500 acres of farmland owned by Kenneth Boening, forty-four, a crop duster and third-generation farmer whose sons will be the fourth generation to till the West Texas soil. Every summer day and most afternoons after school, the younger son, Scott, fifteen, is driving a tractor, cutting and hauling hay, milking cows, cleaning up. After he shared his feelings about his father, he left to make repairs on top of the barn. Then the brawny, leathery, tanned Mr. Boening, drinking reheated black coffee, was interviewed while his wife of twenty-five years—a farm girl who grew up three miles away—worked the CB radio in the office.

I worked *under* my father when I was young; my father never treated me as an equal [said Kenneth Boening]. That was his German way: do it my way, and *only* my way. That's the way my father was. But when my brother and I started farming on our own, my father was real helpful in decision making. If we wanted to buy a piece of land or something we'd ask his advice. I don't say it was always good, but it gave us encouragement. He has a nervous problem now, and he doesn't like to make decisions anymore. He comes up here when he feels like working and now he just feels kinda hurt if he doesn't get to drive the big tractor.

In the period when I worked under my father I think the relationship between us was too distant. It shouldn't be that distant. He was a farmer and I was a farmer and I went to him for advice, but we weren't as close as we should have been. Now we are. We're closer now probably than we ever were when I was a little boy. I think my father has mellowed, that's what it is.

With my sons, it's something hard for me. I want to do the same thing—"Do it my way and that's the way it's going to be. We're going to plant corn, we're not gonna plant milo, because I know it's better, and I don't have to explain to you why." I'm inclined to do that, but I hold myself back and say "Now look, *I* think we ought to plant corn, but if y'all want to go plant milo, well that's fine. We'll go plant milo." I have to make myself do this though. I want them to make their own mistakes because I want them with me in the business. I need them, and if they want to stay in farming today it's just about impossible for a young man unless he's got unlimited backing to take off from scratch. The business here is big enough for them and I want to make them feel like it's theirs. When we make money, *we* make money—when we lose money, it's also *we*. What you're inclined to do as a father is think *I* sure have a good crop but *we* had a crop failure. I don't want to be that way. This all has something to do with my father. We had no real working relationship. We didn't have words or anything, but we were just distant. I try to show a little more affection than he did, but it's not really accepted by my sons. My older one especially— you can hardly touch him; you can tell he doesn't feel right about it. But I guess that's the way we raised him. It's *our* fault.

I've seen men that I thought had a good attitude and were morally straight, who had rats for sons. Why? I have noticed one thing: you need to work or do things with a boy. For instance, city fathers will come out here and buy a tractor and a piece of land for their son to farm, and I think that must be very frustrating to the boy. It does more harm than good. The kid doesn't know which end is up. He has to fake it to try to get through. But if his father was out there *with* him it would be different. I don't mean sitting in the house directing things. I mean physically *with* him.

I worked more with my first son than I did with the second one. I'd be with him all summer. We'd get up in the morning and he was right there with me. I might put him on a tractor and not see him for three or four hours, but I'd be the one who'd pick him up off that tractor. I got into flying after the second one was born and during summers I didn't get to spend as much time with him as with the first . . . and it made a difference. The second one is not a leader as much as the first one. He has trouble making decisions and I don't believe it's just his personality. I really blame it on myself for not being out there with him.

Parents set an example. When the first one was real young my wife was fussing at me for something and I can remember when she turned her back, he was sitting in his high chair and he started fussing at me, too. That taught me right quick: he mocked her right to the word. Kids *want* to be led, I think. They don't like to be pushed. They're like a chain. You have to pull them—and believe me, I've pulled. Sometimes I've pushed and I've pushed too hard. I've had my boys up at 2:30 in the morning to go work after they've played a football game at 9:30 at night. I don't think that hurts them, though. When you're young you're made to stretch out.

I think as far as my sons knowing I love them, I've never really thought about it or worried about it. They know. If I gave them a good paddling when they were younger, I think that was showing that I cared. I always explained to them, "It's hard for me to whip you. You don't know how damn hard it is." It'd be a whole lot easier for me to just walk away from it. It's hard. It's like me putting my oldest boy on the crawler tractor when he was a little boy. He was so small he couldn't pull the clutch in, so I'd ride on it and make one round as he made his way into the field. I'd ride until he was away from the fences, out in the field, and then I'd pull the clutch and jump off. He'd steer that thing round and round the field. It was easy to do this as long as I could see him. Then when he went over the hill and I couldn't see him anymore, that damn knot got in my stomach. Okay, he's eight years old, going round and round on a crawler. I tried to pound into his head just a few simple things to do if something went wrong. And I'd just hope he made the right decisions. A lot of friends of mine have lost sons on the farm in accidents. When something like that happens, and a couple days later you turn your son loose on a tractor, well it's harder.

My sons, when they were younger, right before they went to bed, they'd give us a hug but that's about all. I did very little as far as changing diapers and so forth when they were babies. I guess it was the old German tradition more than anything else. I never wash dishes unless I have to. But let's face it: today there's women who come home with a bigger paycheck than men. I don't have anything against it, but I think it makes it very hard on the family. I think it's going to really take some doing to keep the family together, the kids and everything. Because somebody's gotta buckle under, and in the old German tradition the women did. You know what I mean, the man ruled and woman did what she was told. Well, you know, it's pretty hard for a woman to do what she's told when she's bringing home the bigger check. But I don't see anything wrong with it. If a woman can make it, and she's working and the man's working—or not working—yeah, he ought to pitch in and he ought to do whatever has to be done in the house.

Do I think it's unmasculine for a father to be tender with his son? Wellll, . . . yes and no. I mean that's tradition. I think the woman is supposed to do more of that with the children. I'm not ready for that—why, I don't know. It's tradition. I guess I'd accept it if my sons were different when they have kids. . . . No, I *wouldn't* accept it. Let's be honest about it. To me there's a line drawn—the woman's role and the man's role. I don't say you have to be hard as nails, but when the load is put on you, you gotta carry it. My wife can do most anything I can do as far as decision making in running this farm. She's capable. But whenever it comes down to the dirty work I know I have to do it. And believe you me, I don't want to do it. But it's a man's job. If there's a hand that needs to be fired or something, I don't expect my wife to go do it.

If I'd had a little girl . . . yeah, I think I'd be more affectionate to her. I believe I would. I'd probably teach her things around the farm, like how to drive a tractor, but I wouldn't treat her like a *boy*. I wouldn't want her to do physical hard work like hauling hay. She might help with feeding the stock or something, but to handle bales—no, that's not a woman's place.

I was closer to my mother than to my father. I could always talk to Mama. Then Mama would talk to Daddy. My daddy used to do his whipping when he was mad, and that was one thing I decided that I was never going to do with my children. As far as a regular paddling, I wanted to do that when I was in complete control of myself where I could talk to them. And like I say, that's hard. I'll tell you, I've heard a lot of people talk about disciplining kids by just talking to them. Well, everyone I know, they've finally had to put their foot down. Kids need discipline. They *want* a paddling. On a farm you don't have so much of this grounding business— "You can't do this, you can't go visit with friends." I'd rather give the whipping and get it over with because there are too many other things to be doing.

I don't like to discipline with work because the work becomes the punishment, and that's not the point of the whole thing. We do our work because it needs to be done. I remember a few years ago, my oldest son was tending to calves. My wife walked up on him and he didn't know it. He had a calf there that wouldn't eat and he was trying to make it eat. He thought he was by himself, and he was calling that calf everything that you could think of— "You son of a bitch, if you don't eat you're gonna die!" And he was just crying and cussing, and he had *never* cussed around his mother and me. And I was proud of him because he was trying to get that calf to live. He wasn't doing it for me, he was doing it 'cause it *needed* to be done. That's the difference.

I'm at the age now where I'm looking forward to grandchildren. I think they can enlighten me, let's put it that way. It'll be a new experience. I can enjoy them and then I can give them back to Mama and Daddy. I'm not gonna give the discipline, the harsh discipline, with my grandchildren. No, *that* goes with being a parent.

My dad and I have a working relationship and then a family relationship [said Scott Boening]. Our working relationship is totally different from our family relationship. When we're working, it's more . . . I guess you'd say professional, and in our family we kind of joke and all. When we work we try to be serious. We're always close when we're working but you know you can't be *real* close because then you won't get anything done.

I think of our relationship as close because if I have a problem I can always work it out with him. He's just . . . I don't know how to say it . . . he's just easy. He's affectionate in his own way. I mean he doesn't show much affection but, like, if I do something wrong he doesn't really yell at me, he'll just make me feel a little bad and make me think about it. This way it makes me think for myself.

I spend a lot of time with him. I always see him, always, every day. Especially in the summer. And usually in the winter if he's not out dusting crops he'll be around the house. I'd like to stay here when I grow up and do the same thing. I don't know if I'll crop dust, but I want to farm.

Maybe I'll be more affectionate if I have sons. It'll depend on what the children are like, what they need. My dad never shows it toward me—he does *sometimes,* but not very much—and I never thought of it as a big deal. I don't wish I had it.

The best thing about my father is that he teaches me. If I do something right, he'll make me feel that I did something right. If I do something wrong, he'll just say, "Well, you learn by mistakes." It seems like I remember better when he tells me that I did it wrong and then explains it out. It really teaches me more than anything.

From watching TV and from books I know that back in the 1950s you always heard the mother say, "Wait till Dad gets home." My mom never says that unless she's really, really mad at me. She'll say, "I'm gonna have to talk to your dad about this."

Most of my friends have good relationships with their fathers, too, because this is mostly a farm community. You always hear them talk about their fathers, and what they did today and all. I know a few kids from the city and I guess they don't seem as close to their dads. That's probably because they don't spend much time with them. I don't know when I'd see *my* dad if I didn't work with him.

I don't do much in the house. I try my best not to! Oh, there's nothing wrong with a man doing it. I think it's right for the man to help out with the children now because the mother has a lot more to do, too. My mom does a *lot*. I mean, she'll go out to the barn and go check cows and stuff like that.

I don't think I'll ever leave the farm. I like it. You get to work with people. I am always around with people. We have about ten farm hands. It's an experience for me. I cut hay and haul it with the farm hands, or milk cows, clean up, things like that. My dad started teaching me when I was real young. I was about four or five when I started driving a tractor. It was nothing big. You just drove and you stopped, and drove and stopped. I can basically do most of what my dad does, except not as good. I can't fly yet but I'll learn.

My father's role . . . well, he's more patient. He'll be patient with me just about no matter what. But Mom, she'll haul off and yell and everything. Maybe when I was younger I was closer to my mom 'cause I didn't do as much with my dad. I spent more time with her.

The things that make a good father are just that he should love you, and when you make a mistake he should accept it—I don't mean let it go by. He should make it clear that you did something wrong. I feel that's a good characteristic of my father's. I think the things that make a good mother are similar, in a way. They're really about the same!

16

A graduate of Yale and Harvard Business School and a veteran of banking and corporate finance, Marne Obernauer, Jr., thirty-seven, joined his father six years ago at the Devon Group, Inc., a publicly held wine and spirits and graphic arts corporation headquartered in a spare, sleek suite of offices on Park Avenue. When the senior Mr. Obernauer made the decision to serve solely as chairman of the board last year, his son was elected chief executive officer.

I think the changes that have occurred over the years in relationships between fathers and children have been pretty much dictated by the times, and I don't see how they could have been any different [said Marne Obernauer, Sr.]. The custom when I was a young boy was to spend Saturday afternoons on a baseball field rather than with your father; you saw him at the dinner table or perhaps on some Saturday outing. I have the impression that in my father's time things weren't nearly as enlightened as in my generation. For instance, I can't remember my father being concerned about what college I might be able to get into, but then all it took to get in was a check for $400 and a pulse rate. When I was in college my parents visited and were with me continually during their visit. When I visited my children, I think I was much more aware of scheduling and activities that I didn't want to interrupt. I was content with meeting them for dinner, and wouldn't have *thought* of spending the afternoon or evening with them because that would have been imposing. Therein lies the difference between the two generations.

I would say my son Marne's relationship with his children is much more intimate than mine was. Both he and his wife devote most of their nonworking hours to their children. I admire both my son and my daughter for their relationships with their children, and I happen to be blessed with four wonderful grandchildren as a result.

In some respects my son and I are closely involved, in other respects, no. He never set out to work with me in business. He graduated from Yale and Harvard and became a bank officer and then joined an investment banking firm on Wall Street. He was on his way with his career. At a particular point, I needed someone who had the exact qualifications *he* had. I discussed it with him; he did not embrace the idea immediately. In fact, he turned me down three times. When I owned a very large wholesale distributing operation on the West Coast, Marne consistently refused to become associated with me in the business because he wished to remain in the East. I remember the night I called to tell him I had sold it. His response was, "Now I don't have to feel guilty anymore." His guilt never made him succumb, of course. Anyway, after a while he decided to join forces with me here. We have never worked together as such, however. We've worked for the same purpose, but we've never done it in the same room and we've never done it in the same area of responsibility. In the course of a week, there are more days when we're not in communication than when we are. I'm often out of the office, or he is. I will look in his room before leaving to say good night if he happens to be in, and he'll do the same.

I can't point to much of a problem working with Marne although I must say I have always been aware of some of the problems visited on other father-son relationships in business. I have tried over the years to avoid falling into troublesome patterns that shouldn't come between *any* employees, but particularly between fathers and sons because it spills over into their personal lives. I respect his abilities. I think those areas in which he has expertise exceed my own, whereas I might have a little edge on him with experience in things that relate to past years or past associations. But I would find it very hard to favor a son over another employee, because I think it would create an uncomfortable atmosphere.

My feeling is that the role of the father should always be that of a friend who doesn't get in the way.

I love being a father [said Marne Obernauer, Jr.]. I think it's probably the single most important thing a man can do. We all talk about what we can do, what we can leave to the world. If you believe in values and moral principles, then the most important thing you can do for the world is leave other people who share them.

There are two separate things I love: one is the philosophical satisfaction of having children, and the other is just the day-to-day kinds of satisfactions of watching them grow. There are funny moments and there are difficult moments—we had one last night. My oldest son wouldn't go to bed. It was just a minor discipline problem, but there is a feeling of satisfaction over managing those moments. My wife and I don't always agree. We agree in a general direction, I guess, but we have a difference as to where the limits are. He reached my limit and not hers, and I got *enormous* satisfaction out of resolving the problem; it's a sharing of love.

I express my love in lots of ways. There are physical ways, a lot of touching, kissing, hugging, and there is what I just described— managing the difficult moments. You can't do that without love. It's very easy to lose your temper and just say, "Get out of here." But that's not what you do. I think you're expressing love when you guide them. They learn what it is they did wrong, and what it is that's right.

I'd call my relationship with my father very good. Over the last six years that we've been working together, our level of trust has increased as we've gotten to know what to expect from each other, and how each operates. We have a better idea of how to read each other, which we had never done in a professional sense prior to that. We really had not spent all that much time together since I graduated from high school. I grew up in Pittsburgh, and I went to college at Yale and to business school at Harvard. When I was away at college I was home for vacations and that's about it. Soon after I graduated my parents moved off to the West Coast where my father had a business opportunity. He found himself in New York from time to time on trips, but really it wasn't until we got together in 1974 that we began to see an awful lot of each other.

I've never talked to him about any philosophical views of fatherhood. I guess I never felt the need to. I've always felt very secure that his feelings about his children were of wanting the very best for them, of almost placing us ahead of himself. He's a different father than I will probably be in many ways, because we're products of different backgrounds. He is what people typically refer to as a self-made man. I work hard, but with some relaxation. I can afford to make sure that my family is proximate to my work, and I have the luxury of structuring my work habits even though the hours may run a little long. My father was hustling to such a degree that he had to be on the road an enormous amount of time, so he didn't have that luxury of having his family where he wanted them. I think he has a shorter temper than I have because he drove himself to fatigue.

When we lived in Pittsburgh my father did a lot of traveling to New York City, and I've always thought one of the reasons we didn't move to New York to make life a little easier is because my parents thought it was not the right environment for kids. They couldn't maintain the life-style they had in Pittsburgh in New York. I can afford now to live in Manhattan and have a lot of space and send my three-year-old to nursery school at Park Avenue Christian. Those things are expensive, and I know what a hardship it would have been for my father. Our life-style dovetails with my wife's career, too—she is a vice-president of a large bank on Wall Street—so where we live is convenient to where we work. People will ask me questions about our sharing in child rearing as though it's a hardship or a burden for me, that I should have to do 50 percent of the work. It's not only not a hardship, it's a *joy*. It's better for the kids this way, because they have the benefit of both parents and not one or one and a half.

My wife is a very different kind of woman from my mother. My father was clearly the master of the house. He was a very strong personality; my mother was not. She was what I would describe as a typical wife of that era. Her perceived role was to raise the children and have the house in order, and that was her career. As I think about it, it is a much maligned, an unfairly maligned career. My father's needs were paramount to her, except where they conflicted with the children's needs.

As I went through college in my early twenties, I was not very emotionally or physically expressive. I don't know if that was immaturity or what, but in many ways I have the feeling that what is called women's liberation is basically men's liberation. Men have been liberated from a lot of the stereotypes and hang-ups they had. Certainly one of the things I've been liberated from is any inhibition I might have had about being physically expressive.

Some of the changes we see in our society have been so major that you have to make sure the pendulum doesn't swing too far. One of the things my wife and I had to talk about when we considered marriage was this whole issue of children. She had pretty much come to the conclusion that she was going to live a life without children. Her mother was the perfect mom, and my wife's attitude was that you either do it that way or you don't. We had many talks where I expressed my feelings about the importance of children, and I had some success in convincing her. I wouldn't have tried to convince her if I hadn't thought she would be a super mother, and if I hadn't already seen her interact with children.

149

Here was a great potential mother saying, "I don't think I'm going to have children." It was almost as if the changes in society had gone so far as to make her think she *couldn't* have them.

Male liberation makes my life so much happier because I'm more involved with my children. It also makes my wife so much happier. It gives her such total satisfaction, and that in turn makes *my* life happier. This certainly would have been very difficult in my father's era because of the stereotypes, of the manner in which society would frown upon both men and women altering their roles. Even today, notwithstanding the options for women, if a man decides to stay home and run the house, we frown on that. A househusband is sort of a derogatory term. And if that's true today, think of what it would have been like for a househusband twenty or thirty years ago.

I sometimes ask myself whether I'm doing some rationalizing, because if there's one thing I remember with dissatisfaction it was the relationship between my father and mother as I grew up. My father's domination and my mother's subservience—living to make sure that everything was in place for *him*. It was something I was never comfortable with. I explain the situation in sociological terms, but I sometimes ask myself if I'm rationalizing away any resentment I have toward my mother and father for doing that. I think ultimately it probably contributed to their splitting up. After twenty years together, they separated. It's sad—it's very sad—when society is structured in that way.

To me, the key element in the success of my working relationship with my father is that I came into our partnership at a point where I was not an apprentice. I didn't go into a family business right out of college, as a neophyte. I certainly had a lot of learning to do, and I still do, but I spent five years at a major bank in the city, and two more years at business school, and another two and a half on Wall Street. I was developing skills that were different from my father's. I was coming at things from a different perspective, so I had something to bring to the table to add to the many things *he* brought.

We started from a position of mutual respect and trust. Certainly there were things he knew a lot more about than I did, whether it related specifically to the company we were involved in, or general experience he had that I didn't. On the other hand, there were areas where he had *not* had that much experience. I don't think he reacted adversely to taking new advice. I think that at its worst, there were times when he didn't accept my judgment as professional and skilled. If there was an evaluation that involved the opinion of an investment banker, he might ask another investment banker, even though I had worked in that area. But over a period of time he found out that by and large we agreed. It wasn't a conscious thing, it wasn't him saying, "By golly, he's right after all," but he asked the same question twice less and less.

Now, we're all human, and there's got to be some element of competition, but I would say there's probably less competition between him and me than there is between me and some other guy who's not my father, who's not related to me. I guess I never was aware of that conventional perception of father-son relationships. In fact, there's a level of trust between us which is, I'm sure, greater than the trust that any two other professional workers have for each other, whether they be employer and employee, or peers or whatever. It means that either one of us can do or say what we feel without regard to the political ramifications. Between my father and me, there's never a feeling of "This could cost me my job," or "I'm gonna get you for that." I do everything I can, even if I don't agree with something he's decided, to make sure that not only is he protected in his position but that it appears I'm 100 percent behind him. And vice versa. There's the classic situation of the guy in the other office who lets me go out, gives me a lot of rope, lets me dangle and then cuts it off. I just know my father won't do that.

151

What I mean is that I don't have to protect flanks. Trust is a very strong element.

I've got some ideas he doesn't agree with, but once we finish airing our disagreements, then we start talking about the kids. His grandchildren are very important to him. He's constantly thinking not only about me, but about my sister, about our welfare. Many times it's expressed in terms of monetary things—"Do the kids have enough? I want to give them some money," or something like that. Other times, it's just, "I want to be with them, I want to see them," so it's expressed on all kinds of different levels.

Many people have told me that when their fathers passed away, there was unfinished business, things they wanted to do that they didn't do, things they feel badly about. I'm sure that in my case, if my father passed away tomorrow, I'd feel badly about the fact that we never talked about exactly what I'm talking about today. But he's gonna be around a long time. And I will see to it that we *do* have that kind of talk.

17

Alastair Stair and his son John are a study in contrasts. The elder Stair—chairman of the esteemed Stair & Co. antique store—is a dapper, refined man of impeccable bearing, precise tailoring and English birth. John Stair is a bearded, burly, gregarious American child of the sixties who favors blue jeans, sweat shirts and the fusty warehouse in which he directs furniture restoration for Sotheby Parke Bernet. For two years John worked in his father's elegant New York store before going out on his own.

I would say I treated my father with a little bit more respect than my son treats me—John treats me as a bit of an amusing, out-of-date old fellow.

My father started this business in 1912 in New York and London simultaneously, and though as a boy I always wanted to go into the British Navy, he said, "Oh no, Alastair, you're going to go into the business," and that was the end of that. I'm very glad of it, because there's not much British Navy *now*, and I'm running a successful business.

My son and I get on well together outside the business. He worked with me in the store for two years, but he's a little independent, and it just didn't work out. One problem we had was that he wouldn't dress properly. Now he's running a restoration workshop for Sotheby's, so it's appropriate to wear a sweat shirt and blue jeans, but I didn't think it was quite the thing to do in a 57th Street shop. John's attitude about it was, "Oh, Dad, people take it for what it's worth, and if they're going to worry about dress, you shouldn't care." I told him, "We have old-fashioned customers, and if they come in and see John Stair dressed like this they'll think *I'm* lax. They'll blame *me* for not telling you that you should wear a collar and tie." It seems a minor thing, but actually that was partially responsible for the breakup.

The other problem is that this is a very difficult business because you have your own taste and you buy what you like and what you think you can sell and you're inclined to be a little uptight if something is bought that you can't understand. And you say, "Where did that come from?" and you're told, "Well, I think it's a wonderful piece of furniture," and you say, "Well, I think it stinks, and I don't like it at all." If you express yourself too vehemently it can cause hurt feelings. I had the same problems with my father. I came into his business in 1932, but I left him in 1937 and went out on my own—as my son did. Then I came back toward the end of the war after I'd done my service. I think I was too young, too impatient. I didn't realize the merits of being able to walk right into a fine business, and I moved too quickly. That's the impetuousness of youth.

My father was very austere. He came from the North of England and everything he did was absolutely correct. It was difficult to work with him. I remember one time when I was about twenty-two, I went up to the North and bought a set of chairs and brought them back in the station wagon with me. I sold them the next day for about three times what I paid for them. Now these were the Depression days so that was pretty good. A couple of days later I told my father about the transaction, and instead of praising me for the profit I'd made—which was quite difficult to make in 1933–34—he said, "You fool, you should never have sold those chairs for that amount of money." He expressed himself very vehemently and was intolerant of my lack of knowledge and he hurt my feelings deeply.

When my son and I had our disagreement, I was probably as vehement, yes. I tried to modulate myself a bit but I might have been a little too expressive. John is a very hard-working young man. He's very positive, very sure that everything he does is right. And when we didn't agree, it was just better to terminate our business relationship. It was seven or eight years ago that he left. I was very upset, because I had great hopes for him being able to take over the business.

But I'm very proud of John. He's the kindest fellow; he does more for other people than anybody I've ever known—sometimes too much. He's very good with his children, a devoted father. He takes a lot of interest in them. He's divorced, and the other day his wife was away and he took over his two children and his stepson. He was baby-sitting for the three of them. I don't think I would have done that when I was his age. It's to my detriment to say it, but I don't think I was as interested in him as he is in his children. I went through a divorce when he was a young boy. I sent John to England to live with my parents because I couldn't cope. You have to work long hours in this business. In those days I was working six days a week, so it was difficult to keep him.

I felt respect for my father, but not a terrific amount of love. He was rather cold and I hardly ever saw him. I was born and brought up in England, and I went to boarding school when I was eight years old. Even when I wasn't in school, my father didn't come home from work until seven o'clock or 7:30. By that time, I was about to be put to bed. He played golf every Saturday and Sunday, so I didn't see him very much. I had respect and affection for him, but we weren't very close. He'd put his arms around me occasionally and things like that, and tell other people what a fine son I was—I did well in school, I was a good athlete and did all the right things—but he was not open, he didn't tell me to my face what he thought of me. I think he loved me deeply, but he was very undemonstrative, very taciturn. He didn't show much affection for my mother either, and they were married for forty-eight years. He didn't display his emotions like most fathers would.

If I could have changed it, I would have made more effort to get closer to him. I'd have asked him to take me out when he was playing golf, and things like that. If I could have foreseen the future that I had with him, I'd have gotten to know him better. I'd have spent more time with him. I'd have worked harder at it than he worked with me. He was a very good golfer and I'd just taken up golf, and he'd say, "Well you don't play with a pro, Alastair." I never played with him because he was intolerant of my lack of ability at the game. If I could have said to him, now Dad, you've got to teach me—but that's hindsight.

I guess I've somewhat duplicated him in my relationship with John, yes. I would change that now, too. I wouldn't have sent him to school in England. I'd have made every effort to keep him with me, because he lived with my parents during the holidays and he didn't have too much of a home life. They lived way out in the country and there weren't many children around and I don't think he had too happy a holiday period. If I'd had him with me, we'd have been closer together.

I have a stepson also, a most devoted stepson. He's done everything absolutely correctly. I sold this business a year ago, and Bill, who's a Harvard graduate and Fulbright scholar, handles my finances and calls me up every other day and says, "How are you, Dad?" and everything like that. When I married his mother Bill was eight years old, and he is really closer to me than my son, who was with his mother a lot and went to school in England. So we got separated and my stepson took his place. But I think basically the father-son relationship is improving.

My stepson, who is a great sailor, has a 36-foot sailboat and he goes off sailing with his wife and two children—one is four and the other seven—for two weeks at a time. They go to places like Nantucket, and they've got a wonderful relationship with their children. I think it's great. It gives the children stability.

I enjoy being with my grandchildren—for a period of time. We have a house up in the country and they come and spend one weekend a month with us. I think I'm more demonstrative with my grandchildren than I was with my children. In England one went to boarding school and had a flock of servants and nurses and things like that. There's more of a family relationship over here, I think, than there was in England.

I think the mistakes with my father taught me a great deal. I hope John has learned from his. He joined the Marines when he was eighteen, after an unpleasant altercation with me that encouraged him to join. He is a smart fellow, but he didn't work hard enough in school. So I raised hell, and he said, "Well, I think it would be a good idea if I joined the Marines." I said, "I think it would, too." I believe it did him a lot of good, because he saw the rough aspects of life. I served in the British Army before the war, and in the Canadian Air Force during the war. These military experiences influenced me a great deal. I had led quite a sheltered life, and mixing with the rough-and-ready type did me a lot of good.

I guess neither John nor I are demonstrative with each other, but I'm sure he loves me. I love him too. I think he and I are basically very similar. Sometime soon—maybe after this conversation—I'm going to get a little closer to him. You've made me feel I've been a little negligent. You've made me think about something I didn't quite realize: John's affection for *me*.

I was sent to live with my grandparents in England when I was seven, and after that I never really lived at home again [said John Stair]. I don't remember an awful lot about my father before that. I always went away to school because my father believes as many English do that the only education is an English education. I had very little contact with him when I was in England—vacations, basically.

My grandparents were very nice, but they were also aloof. It wasn't like growing up in an American family where you're very close. I had a professional nanny and there was a downstairs maid and upstairs maid—it was a pretty grand style. They lived in a big eighteenth-century house, my grandmother in one end and my

159

grandfather in the other. The only time we ever met was for meals. The dining room happened to be right in between. My grandmother would come in from this way, my grandfather from that way, and then they'd go back to their separate quarters. There was real love, but it was an aloof type of love. In the English system, you have a child, you love the child—I'm sure as much as anyone in America—but you turn it over to a nanny. I had a tremendous amount of respect for my grandparents, but I don't recall hugging and kissing my grandfather, and there was very little of that with my father. I think that's more English than American, too. I'm much more American. I'm big on hugging my children—it's totally natural for me. My father is reasonably good with my children, but there's no hugging or anything. He's not a children kind of person. He's busy twenty-four hours a day. He's a big socialite, which I hate. Of course I knew he loved me. Maybe it's just an assumption on my part, but I always felt a warmth . . . it just wasn't a hugging, American kind of warmth.

I never really had any contact with my father until I worked for him. When I got back from England I spent four years in the Marines, and by the time that was over I was interested in the art business and I went to London for a training program at Sotheby's, So after the age of seventeen I wasn't dependent on my father at all. I changed radically in the service. My family had always had a reasonable life-style, with a nice big apartment in Sutton Place. From that, at the age of seventeen, I went off to Parris Island. You wake up the next morning with your head shaved, and four months later you're still marching in circles with a whole bunch of people from West Virginia. There were two guys who had to be taught how to tie their shoelaces. From New York to basic infantry is a big change, and you grow up real fast. I decided during those four years that I wanted to make a living in architecture. So in Cambodia, when everyone was reading *Playboy*, I was reading about Chippendale highboys. When I started at Sotheby's I was the only American working there, and I don't think I could have taken the

160

abuse without the Marine Corps training. Everything after that was easy. Today I love what I do. I get up every morning and get to the shop at 7:30 and I'm here until 6:00 or 6:30. If I didn't have a family, I'd be here twenty-four hours a day.

I think I worry more about my children today than my father did when I was growing up. I have two sons, nine and thirteen, by my first wife, and a stepson who is seven. My thirteen-year-old has a friend up in the country where we have a summer home, and one day he came over stoned. All of a sudden it hit me. My child was the same age as this boy who was smoking pot. That kind of thing really worries me.

I let my children work in the shop with me. All three of them worked here this week, sweeping and cleaning, and it was really neat. The more time they spend here, the more they understand it, and the more they can appreciate it. This is a great place for children, with the workshop downstairs and tons of blocks and nails and hammers. They spent a whole Saturday building something. And when they understand what goes into polishing a piece of furniture and changing the color of a piece of wood or restoring a bronze, their whole attitude changes. I think now they look on the objects they have at home with more respect. Actually what's happening to them is the same thing that happened to me. You do pick it up. At home I was told, "Don't put your Coke on the table; that's a 200-year-old Georgian piece, and you should respect it. Don't lean back in the Chippendale chair." So pretty soon I began to recognize that this shape was Georgian, that style, Chippendale.

I'd like to train my sons in something like this. My father wasn't really involved in the physical aspects of this work. He's a salesman. He is extremely dapper and well dressed, the opposite of me. He has a restoration workshop, but he doesn't run it himself. He's in the retail end of things. I like this much more. It's very satisfying to take an object that looks totally destroyed and make it into something.

161

My only resentment against my father is that he painted a picture of Stair & Co., and what I could become at Stair & Co., and it was evident after the first year that it wasn't true. It was totally my father's fault, which I think he'd admit, too. He'd been running that business by himself for thirty-two years, and after thirty-two years no matter how much you respect your son, it's very hard to relinquish any of the authority. He wouldn't relinquish *any* of it; therefore, I couldn't take over. I'd just come from being on the board at Sotheby's and all of a sudden to work for a gallery in New York with no authority at all was a change I couldn't take. The problem was a difference in taste. I mean, I could buy a seventeenth-century chair and he'd agree it was seventeenth century, but because he didn't like it he'd let me know I shouldn't have bought it. You only prove yourself when you turn around and sell it for two or three times what you paid for it. His taste filled that six-story building for thirty-two years, and my taste was different. Maybe I preferred to buy more oak than mahogany. It was a tremendous clash. I went for two years without talking to him.

Now my father and I sometimes turn to each other for judgments. He was definitely a big influence in my life. Even before I went to England, I was aware of good things because of him. My father still thinks I'm too impulsive, and he wishes I dressed better, but I think he respects the rate at which I work. He comes up to my office occasionally and he's fascinated with all the young people around. It's funny: I think we get along better now than we ever have.

18

Fred DiGiulio, thirty-three, works variously as a carpenter, contractor and private detective. A humorous man who frequently bursts into great peals of laughter, he lives in a modest neighborhood in a small frame house liberally cluttered with his son's toys. Mr. DiGiulio shares custody of six-year-old Juan with his former wife.

I guess the birth of my son was the most memorable moment of my life. I imagine once my history is written it'll be the only thing to say. I took the preparation for his birth as seriously as I'd taken anything in my life. Of course when he was born it was a big moment, and now that he's six years old, it seems bigger than anything else. I had hoped fatherhood was going to be this great, this satisfying, this intense, this constant . . . this rewarding. The only thing I knew about raising kids before that came from the experiences of my neighbors. They had a daughter whom they had a horrible relationship with. I disagreed with the way they handled everything, always fighting with their child. They never really put their foot down; there was nothing demanded of her. I knew when Juan was born I was not going to do *anything* the way they did it, but I didn't have a whole lot of confidence that I'd do a lot better. My friends' little girl was very close to me. She knew that I had a minimum standard of behavior when she was around me, and that it stuck. And that was all the discipline I ever had to impose on her. After Juan was born, it was very simple to figure out what he was capable of as far as behavior. We've had an occasional confrontation, but he just wants to make sure that what I have demanded will be enforced—or maybe he's curious to find out in what *way* it will be enforced. What that little girl was doing was begging for her parents to set boundaries for her. She didn't feel as comfortable without boundaries. Children may be able to live in their own world of vagueness, but when their *parents* are vague, that's upsetting.

Juan stays with me half the time. He comes every Saturday, Sunday and Monday, and every other Tuesday. Everything's fifty-fifty with my ex-wife, even money. Actually, he stays with me more, because I rarely require her to take up slack for me. He and I go to Florida at least once a year, and I wouldn't think of going without him. He contributes entertainment to all the time we spend together. He's part of the fun and part of the responsibility.

My ex-wife is about to remarry, and there is always the possibility that they will decide to move. Or what would be worse, though it's a remote possibility, is that they could become fanatics of some type. Of course that would be *horrible.* If he was moved away from here, Juan just wouldn't have the variety he has in his life now. He's got cousins and uncles all around him, and he's friends with many adults.

My father and I were affectionate with each other, but not to the extent that Juan and I are. Well, for one thing I had three brothers, and the oldest of us was only six and a half years older than the youngest, and there was a lot more confusion and a lot less time for each individually. There was a lot of *routine* affection. If my father was leaving town—which he did quite often because he was a geophysicist and traveled all over the world—everybody got a big kiss and a hug, even when we were fifteen, and even now. Even now. I think maybe he's less affectionate than most Italian Americans. You know, brother and brother kiss—you saw it in *The*

Godfather. I like that. But I think my being affectionate with Juan doesn't have anything to do with being Italian. It has as little to do with the way I was raised as spanking him does. I think it has to do with how our relationship started, and how it went on. He used to spend a lot of time in my lap, and on my stomach. I would rock him to sleep at night, a real routine we had when he was just a little baby. And I even sing to him now. It got to where we were really openly affectionate, a lot of kissing and hugging throughout the day. It's not uncommon for us to ask for affection, just ask for it if we want some. I do it more than he does. I'll say, "Come here and give me a kiss, give me some love." And he never hesitates. Sometimes I realize that he has something else on his mind; he's a little too much in a hurry and he'll give me a quick peck and that's it. He doesn't spend as much time on my lap anymore, and he's never slept with me. It seems the older he gets, the less of that he wants or needs. But me, I kind of stay the same. I'd like as much affection as I used to have. He now accepts a lot of offers to be away from here or from his mother's house. He's getting very independent, and I think he's probably going to be satisfied with less time with me. But our time is all good time. You know, I never baby-sit him. He's *with* me, we're with each other, we're father and son, and we're *supposed* to be there. We spend our time in a good mood. I love that one-on-one closeness I have with my son. That's probably the best part of fatherhood.

My father and I didn't have anything like the relationship I have with my son, really. There were so many times when he wasn't around. For a period of many years, he was out of town more than he was in town. He was a workaholic. He tried to do a little bit of everything, but he just didn't have the time. For instance, when we went on a rare vacation or an outing, like swimming, we all felt very close, and it was a hell of a lot of fun. He was a hell of a dad. He would deal with all four of us for hours and hours, all day long, he was always all-gang, all play. But that was rare.

If I could have made anything different, I would have corrected

167

that one thing—I would have had my father spend more time with us, more time at home. He would change that, too. He's said it before: that he just missed all that time with us without really realizing he was missing it, thinking that he was working toward earning that time or something. And the realization came too late. That's not the case with Juan and me. We're really best friends.

I've been warned by people older than me that when a man's son reaches a certain age it's hard to be friends anymore. But I've seen that that's not necessarily the case. I'm friends with a man of forty-seven who plays on the softball team. He's got three sons. His oldest son is about twenty-five, his youngest about twenty, and they're all really good friends with him. In fact, it's uncanny. They look like they've always seen eye to eye on everything.

A good father, I think, would be any man whose child says, "I've got a good daddy." I would say that about my own father, and I hope Juan would say it about me. When I think of father-son relationships I think of fun and laughter. I think it's very flattering that this little child loves you so much, and thinks you're the greatest person in the whole world. He would rather have *you* than Superman and all other men combined. He would bank his money on having you fight Muhammad Ali and Godzilla at once—he knows you could figure something out. Hopefully I'll never be too big a disappointment. You know, I used to go out walking in the woods a lot and as I was wandering around I would knock over dead trees. Well one day I took Juan and some of his friends along and I pushed over a dead tree for them, for all these kids. From that day on I was the strongest dad in the world. I became his superhero.

19

Photographer James Mitchell,* a rangy thirty-eight-year-old with angular features and a reticent disposition, was reared on a farm in Wisconsin but now resides on the West Coast. Mr. Mitchell has joint custody of his eleven-year-old son, Brett.

I see my father only once or twice a year. He's a farmer who lives in Wisconsin, and I live in California—but then I moved to California so I wouldn't have to be around him that much. I'm an only child and my parents always expected too much of me, expected me to be the person they wanted me to be. They wanted me around all the time—they're used to being around *their* parents. It just feels too claustrophobic with them. When you're close you have to talk, and I just didn't have much to talk about with them. It is the difference in our life-styles; they're more conservative. Neither of them went to college, and I have a different outlook on things, different interests.

There were times I felt close to my father, like when he took me hunting and fishing. I felt closest to him then because he was really in charge, he knew what he was doing, he was very willing to teach me. It felt really good, knowing he was in charge of everything that could possibly happen. Now he's in charge of his own little world, and it is very narrow. As long as I related to him in his area, things were okay. But that felt really limiting to me.

My father was not physically demonstrative with affection. He never would touch me. I think that would have been so nice; I missed that. Neither of my parents was physically affectionate toward me or toward each other either. I knew they loved each other, but they had this idea that you just don't show affection in front of other people—including the kids.

I touch my son a lot more. I hug him a lot and do father-son things—playing baseball, that kind of thing. And I try to expose him to more things than my father knew about. If my son is interested in piano I encourage him to take lessons. I try to give him a broader view of things.

I knew my father had a way of coping—when something would happen he had a way of dealing with it. And it's that kind of role model that I'm trying to show Brett—that I can handle all situations when they come up, and if I don't know the answer to something I will have ways of finding out. If he asks, "What are the northern lights?" I don't just say "I don't know," I show him ways of finding out how you get that kind of information.

I see my son half the time. He's with his mother one week and with me one week. Sometimes I think I'd like to be there more for Brett. It doesn't seem as if half the time is very much. He basically *lives* with his mother and *visits* me, so many of the decisions about his schooling and where he's going to spend his time are made by her. She and I don't communicate too well anymore, so she just goes ahead and makes a lot of those decisions.

As Brett has gotten older he seems to need more from me and less from her. When I express an interest in something, in a couple of days *he's* interested in it and he wants information about it. He's patterning himself after me a little. I've always been interested in sports, and now *he's* interested in sports. I came back from Alaska interested in the northern lights, and then *he* wanted to know about them. He sees the stuff I do and copies that—as I did with my dad.

As I got older, I identified more with my father than with my mother. When I was younger I needed her a lot more because she took care of those younger-child needs. Then as I got older I needed my dad more because he was—well, a man in a man's role.

I see a man's role as both the traditional one of being the breadwinner, and then the nontraditional role of also taking part in the housework—cleaning, cooking, and so forth. My father didn't see housework as part of a man's role. I was back home last month and my uncle and his wife were there for dinner. As soon as dinner was over, the two men got up and went off and sat in the living room while the women cleared the table. That's something I've gotten totally away from. That was part of my parents' culture. I'm used to doing my share of all the housework.

My son was two and a half when my wife and I separated, and we divorced about two or three years after that. When he was little I would get up for those two o'clock feedings—I thought it was my responsibility as well as my wife's. I think the father can do just as good a job of rearing a child as the mother. Those things are learned anyway, and there's no reason a man can't learn them just as well as a woman.

I make a conscious effort to be affectionate with my son. If we're sitting on the couch together, for instance, I will consciously put my arm around him and pull him a little bit closer. It's really nice to be a father—it makes life seem permanent and lasting. There's another little person who looks at me and imitates me and I'm one of the most important people in his life. He's only eleven, growing up and about to be a teenager. That's pretty scary, I guess. I started pulling away from my own father before adolescence. When I was around him, my mother talked all the time and my dad didn't talk very much and I would just tune out, space out, think about something else. As I got older and had more independence I would just arrange it so I wasn't around them. When they went to Grandma and Grandpa's house on Sundays, I would find something else to do.

My father always said he wanted me to have a better life than he had. He'd had to work very hard doing physical labor all his life. He knew that it took a toll on him, and he didn't want me to do the same thing. He wanted me to go to college and be an engineer or do some kind of desk thing. I think he respects my profession as a photographer, but he's somewhat afraid for me because I spend a lot of time in planes and helicopters.

My parents do love me a great deal—in fact, I was *smothered* by love. I got too big a dose. They would have been much happier with two or three kids. My father has nine brothers and sisters and my mother's got five so they're used to big families and family closeness. They like having those big tables with fifteen people per meal and somehow they only ended up with one kid. They wish they had more kids who would drop by occasionally so they would have a steady dose of family.

Even I regret that I didn't have brothers and sisters. It would have made things so much easier. With just me there's all this pressure—I am all they've got. So I removed myself to escape the pressures. They used to come to California and I would frequently go to the Midwest for part of the winter, but I don't go back all that often anymore. Our reunions are sort of a ritual. My mother fills me in on all the people who have died or gotten married or had kids and my dad—well, he doesn't say *anything*.

Parent-child needs change over the years. A child of eleven needs a lot more of me than I need of him. But there may be a time as I get older that I need more of him. Like I'm kind of getting the message from my parents that they need more of me as I get older. They would love it if I lived in their town so I could come by and help at, you know, putting up storm windows, putting on a new roof. My dad is getting older and he can't do as much as he once could.

I'm trying to channel my son toward certain things—I'm not just letting him free-flow. And yet I don't want to put too much of my imprint on him, so he can be who he wants to be.

Some of my warmest times with my son are when we go to the country together, to Yosemite, on hikes, or do tasks together like building spaceships. When he was smaller there was a time that I had negative feelings about him. My ex-wife and I weren't getting along too well before he was born, and rather than bringing us together, his birth put a wedge between us that finally forced us apart. So there was resentment on my part, because as an infant he needed so much attention. He had colic, so he needed extra care. I resented that—it wasn't easy for me to deal with that.

I always had the feeling that I had come between *my* parents. I felt like my mother had a lot more affection for me than she showed and that she was unsure about how my dad would feel if she showed affection for me. I always felt like the third person, the sort of odd one. I knew that they had their own bedroom where they slept and then there was me by myself. I felt like I was almost an intruder at times. I think if I had had a brother or sister, I wouldn't have felt so much that way. Brett is also an only child and I wonder if he ever feels the same way. I don't really know.

I never want to have a child from scratch again, but I consider my new girl friend's son Dan a part of my family. He's seventeen, a high school senior. I'm beginning to get really close to him. He's very much interested in mechanics, cars, engineering, and I don't know much about those things. He's different from Brett in that he's got knowledge, so that when I see him I can get information from him. Brett doesn't have that kind of knowledge yet. I see Dan as a potential son, and I definitely like the feeling of there being other people in my family besides one child. Dan is an only child, too, and he's used to being close to his mother, so I'm sure he sees me as somewhat of an intruder. I try to ease that feeling by seeing Carolyn at times when he's around. I would much rather have this boy accept me than just say, "All right, he's part of the family now so make the best of it."

Brett enjoys Dan because he sees how older kids are, and how they react when they're out by themselves and not around their parents. So it's kind of like having an older brother for him. For Dan it's like having an adopted younger brother who's light-years away from him.

I don't think divorce is really too good for kids. A lot of them have a hard time dealing with it. Like with Brett—one week with me, one week with his mother. When I was growing up I always knew where my home was. I knew exactly where to go. I didn't have to think, "This is Monday night, now who's picking me up?" Sometimes my ex-wife and I will make a last-minute arrangement and I'll go pick up Brett and he'll be surprised that *I'm* there. So there's a kind of confusion and splitting apart. He's tiptoeing from one side of the fence to the other. It was really comforting to me growing up knowing my family was solid. Divorces just didn't occur. It was such a secure feeling. I can see a confusion in Brett and other kids. They don't really know what's happening except one of their parents lives in one house, maybe remarried, and the other lives somewhere else. It's gotten easier for Brett now because he's older and can deal with it better. He has a stepfather he's close to and loves now.

I guess it makes me jealous that another man has more time with my son than I do, but I also know that Brett recognizes the difference in our roles. He tells me that he cares for Julian but he knows that *I'm* his father and Julian is his mother's new husband. There's a difference. A father is somebody you look like, who is your own blood, not somebody who only raises you, or cares for you.

It was hard when I first separated because I didn't see Brett that much and he didn't have that assurance that I still cared about him. I know it was going through his head that he had something to do with us splitting up. He wasn't getting very much from me then because I just wasn't seeing him very much. I was trying to get my own life reestablished, moving out of my house, making adjustments, and the idea of joint custody hadn't really occurred to me. I was seeing him maybe on Saturdays and Sundays. One of the good things about joint custody is that I'm not around him so much that I get tired of him. I never wish he were just gone, which I'm sure full-time parents often feel. When I was living with my ex-wife I didn't have any breaks from him. But now I do so that when he's away I miss him.

I find that as he gets older I like him more, because he can handle more of his own stuff. I couldn't stand that diaper-changing stage where he was totally dependent. I can relate to him more as a person, not just as a small creature who needs me. I really wanted a son. I would probably have been disappointed if he had been a girl. I guess that's just traditional. I know that there are some cultures that believe you're not really a man unless you produce male offspring and I see that somewhat in my relatives.

I think my son's feelings about me are mostly favorable. He probably wants me not to lose my temper as much and I guess he wants me around more. But he idolizes me—after all, I'm the only father he's got.

20

Over a hamburger lunch in an airy restaurant set serenely in a Midwest woodland, Dr. John Harrison,* a dentist, and his eleven-year-old son Edward talked—with a healthy dose of jesting banter between them—of their lives together as part of a burgeoning trend in this country, of children living in the custody of their fathers. Some months previously, Edward had chosen to live with Dr. Harrison after spending three years with his mother and younger sister in a Southeast beach town.

Dr. Harrison: My wife and I were divorced about three years ago, and Edward lived with his mother until this past summer. He and I essentially presented her with the fact that he wanted to live with me and she said okay. We've been together now about four months.

Edward: I wanted to live with Dad. I missed him. He's a cool guy, he's nice, and I guess I liked him more than my mother. I feel more like him because he's a male. I'm happier with him, too. He takes me fishing and hunting and we do the same things. And he's got a good personality and a sense of humor. He's understanding. He's a good father. The only time he's not is when he tells me I can't handle poisonous snakes. I mean, it's *my life.*

Dr. Harrison: I would describe myself as a little over-indulgent as a father. This is probably still the honeymoon stage with him, so I'm not as strict as I should be. I'm very aggressive about spending time with him and always have been—doing things with him, teaching him things, getting him interested and active in a variety of things. We have our outdoor activities together, we build and make things together, like treehouses. I get him to read and listen to music. I pick him up from school every day and I try not to go back to the office. I prefer to be with him. I think fathers *should* spend time with their children, but more important is that I like doing it. My own father did the same thing with me. We engaged in identical sorts of activities, either going on trips, or building something, or doing things around the house, or hunting and fishing. I was in boarding school, so that probably eliminated a lot of the time I could have spent with him. In Australia it's a privilege to go to boarding school—here it's often because your parents don't want you around. I felt a sense of responsibility because my parents had financially gone out of their way to let me go to boarding school to get a better education.

I'm also very physically affectionate with Edward, to the point that it becomes a problem.

Edward: Yeah, I don't like men touching me. I'm not the type. I'll touch girls, but not men.

Dr. Harrison: I'm your *father*. That's a different category altogether. If a father loves you he can touch you, can't he?

Edward: Not *me*.

Dr. Harrison: I participated in the early stages of his life. The only thing I wouldn't do is change a really dirty nappy; I'd change the wet ones but not the dirty ones. I'd feed him, because he was bottle fed.

The interesting thing will be when I see a lot more independence in Edward—that's what really worries me, how to keep some kind of control. There's the anxiety that he'll do something destructive to himself like trying to fly out of a tree. I'm trying to teach him things that relate to people and automobiles and sex and drugs.

Edward: What have you told me about trucks?

182

Dr. Harrison: No, *drugs*.

It was very lonely when he was living with his mother, and I missed him. I was always more involved with my children than their mother. It was very rare to have a whole-family activity going on. If we wanted to go to the park or skiing or to the tennis courts, she'd say, "Go on, I'm not feeling well," or something.

Edward: She was a pain in the butt.

Dr. Harrison: What about when you lived with her, didn't she do anything?

Edward: She'd take us to the beach, but she wouldn't do anything. She'd just sit there.

Dr. Harrison: Both my wife and I were keen on children early on, but we had to put it off because of medical school, and by the time we had our first child I think she might have been less interested; I think she regarded it as an imposition. It was probably strategically a pity it was delayed quite as much as it was. But Edward was the perfect son. He's outgoing . . .

Edward: What's outgoing?

Dr. Harrison: You talk to people, you're friendly, you're fun to be with. You're a joy to be with all the time.

He's very seldom miserable. Occasionally he'll get miserable but generally he's good and positive and doesn't carry a slight too long. If I reprimand him he'll be upset for a little while and then it's over.

I'll tell you some bad things about him, too. He's getting rotten grades in school.

Edward: Oh, that's nothing.

Dr. Harrison: What do you mean it's *nothing?*

Edward: I wouldn't worry about it.

Dr. Harrison: You wouldn't worry about it? You're gonna be digging ditches when you grow up.

Edward: So I will.

Dr. Harrison: But he can do a lot better than he's doing. I'm delighted the way his music is coming along. He's in the school band now, and I think that's tremendous. He's developing the same interests I have. But I think it's pretty hard for a father to artificially create an interest, to say, "I think it would be wise for you to be interested in golf." Inevitably we tend to foster our *own* interests. I hope he's inherited some of my perseverance, though.

Edward: What's that? Hey, hey, hey! hang on! What do you mean by that?

Dr. Harrison: To stick at something.

Edward: Oh yeah, to stick it to you.

Dr. Harrison: No, no, not to stick it to you.

And to try to have a broad range of interests rather than to be interested in just one area. He'll probably be more interested in sports than I was.

Edward: I *am*.

Dr. Harrison: I *know* you are.

Edward: I bet when you were eleven you couldn't do 300 pounds. I'm not bragging, but . . .

Dr. Harrison: You can do 300 pounds?

Edward: On the leg lifts. That's a lotta leg.

I'll tell you what I hope I inherit from my father: the *money*.

Dr. Harrison: I hate to tell you, but we don't have any. Mum took it all.

I envy Edward's ability to meet people and immediately communicate with them. It's something I don't do well. His genuine interest and concern and involvement with people is a very positive thing. And everything else about him is neat.

Edward: Perfect.

[Have you ever seen your father cry?]

Edward: Only when a girl dumps him.

Dr. Harrison: Every night.

Edward: Daddy, you just took my joke! And, he cries when he looks at his bank account. I saw him cry when I was little.

Dr. Harrison: You did?

Edward: Can I say this?
Dr. Harrison: Sure.
Edward: He cried when his brother died.
[What do you think about men who cry?]
Edward: Why *can't* they cry?

21

Reared in a Mexican-American border town, Victor Garcia,* an angelic-faced twenty-seven-year-old, now lives on the East Coast, where he is employed in a restaurant. He is unmarried.

I never really knew my real father. My stepfather married my mother when I was six and from that time on we were enemies. We just never got along. I was always very rebellious—if he said red, I said green. I always did what I wanted to do, and he felt that he could never really control me. And he wanted that. I see it happening now with my sisters—he has them under his control. And so we always went against each other; we always used to fight.

He met my mother when I was about five and a half. Until then I had been alone with her. We were very close, and then after that I was like separated from my mother. Then she had my sisters—I have five—and we became more and more distant. Because of that I left home at a very early age—thirteen and a half.

One day I was getting dressed for school, and I was so sick and tired of arguing, I wasn't happy at all. I played hooky and came home around noon through the backyard and I heard my stepfather say, "Just wait till Victor gets home," and I had heard him say

"Wait till Victor gets home" so many times that I'd had it. So I took whatever I could find and I left. I moved in with another family, who kind of adopted me. I didn't see my parents for four years. I just disappeared. And then I came to New York when I turned seventeen, and they didn't even know.

I have a lot of friends who have recently become fathers, and they are really participating in bringing up the children. I think that's fabulous. I wish I had had somebody to guide me. Actually, my stepfather tried to do that. I spent a lot of time and energy hating him, but one day I woke up and said, "Why am I spending all this time hating him when he was *trying* to be a father, whatever that means?" Nobody ever wrote a book for him on how to be a parent, on what to do, on what it means. I spent all this time hating him for doing things he thought were correct. I wanted the guidance, but because I was strong and had my own feelings, sometimes I felt that guidance was interfering with what I wanted to do. But I got no warmth and affection, none at all.

When I left home, I had to learn everything by myself, I had to educate myself, I had to experience everything myself. I dropped out of school at fourteen and I liked being out, I liked being by myself. I was once so close to my mother and sisters that if someone had told me I was going to leave Laredo and go to New York, I would have said, "That's impossible." That's why now it's so wonderful. They see that I have made a life of my own and they're really very happy for me. And now my stepfather is my best friend. I go back to visit them every year, and about two years ago he took me aside and told me he was very proud of me, that I had made a success of myself. Because when I left home, they figured, "Well, Victor, forget it." It's fabulous for me, because now I'm really close to them.

I tend to be overly generous with my sisters now, since I remember what it was like back then for me. We were really poor. It was so horrible. I used to cry out of anger because I couldn't escape it. I was trapped by poverty. I couldn't *change* anything.

When I left home all I had was fifty cents and a few clothes, and that's it. It was lonely, very lonely. I remember one time after I left I was standing on a street corner and I was too proud to go home. My stepfather would never have let me live it down. I couldn't go back until I had something to show for myself. It was just before I met the family I stayed with, and I had no money and no place to go and I thought, How horrible! I'm standing here by myself and I have no one to turn to.

If I had children I would try to be understanding of things. That's so important. And I would try to guide them but also give them the freedom to find themselves. I guess that's it: My stepfather was trying to guide me, but he didn't give me the freedom to find myself. He tried to mold me. We would have terrible battles, going at each other, and I remember my mother watching and I would feel bad for her because she would watch him kick me and she couldn't do anything. She was married to him and she couldn't say, "Don't slap him," because he would turn on *her*. So she never said anything.

I didn't feel any resentment toward her, really. I felt more hurt by both of them, because I always wanted to be loved and I was being pushed further and further away. That's why it's so wonderful now. We have a lot of communication and that's what I always wanted. It's like I've found my family again.

22

Patrick Hemmings,* a thirty-five-year-old supervisor for a major construction company, lives with his wife and year-old daughter in a cozy bungalow in New Jersey. An articulate, intelligent man dressed in Brooks Brothers collegian style, his conversation spans a wide range of interests—from literature to business to sports to philosophy.

The one occasion that I can recall my father ever touching or putting his arm around me was when I was in the seventh grade. He'd just gotten out of the hospital after a lengthy illness He was going to surprise my sister and me by hiding in the bedroom, but when we got home from school he just couldn't keep the suspense up. As soon as we opened the door he rushed over and grabbed us, with tears coming down his cheeks, and I can remember the scratchy stubble on his face when he hugged us. I remember that feeling and I remember him crying. It only lasted about thirty seconds. That is the one and only time in my life he ever really touched me. We never even shook hands until recently. It's not his way. He is incapable of expressing any kind of physical tenderness. I think that was just part of this Irish thing; my grandfather never touched either. There was always some sort of a masculine code, a tacit understanding that men who did that were faggots, or that it just wasn't a manly thing to do. Any kind of masculine affection was basically a taboo. But it was a tacit taboo; it was never really stated.

Money was the preferred form of expression. By the time I was six years old I had everything I ever wanted. My grandfather, who was a very wealthy man, was still very much in the picture at this time. We went to his house two or three times a week, and he would always give me money. It was ridiculous. Every day while my father was away, my grandfather would give me a dollar—in the early fifties a dollar was like ten bucks today. Somehow or other I just understood that the men in my family were very clumsy emotionally, and this was the best they could do. They were locked into behavior patterns that did not permit them to express affection in any other way except showing largesse.

The other thing is that the women were always tremendously affectionate, which is something that still hangs me up today. I do not like to be touched. I was touched too much by my mother and grandmother. They were the type of people who could not talk to you without constantly grabbing your hand. I was always smothered by women when I was growing up, and I have this terrible ambivalence about the women's movement as a consequence. In my family, and I think in most Irish families, women have all the power. I saw it very early on, and it continued right through my adolescence; all the power was held by the women.

I touch my own child, but I think that's a function of my recent growth and my marriage. Before that I was very reticent about showing any kind of affection toward children or being demonstrative in any way. I still feel that way a bit. What it's made me think about with this whole masculine-feminine polarity is that men have been conned too long by women. If you look at the society I grew up in, the women didn't have to work. They got to sit around and play bridge, and had servants to do everything. The whole housework issue seems totally irrelevant to me. The women had everything and had it completely made. They just sat back and ran the show while the men did their macho stuff. I remember it used to be great fun when I was growing up to go to the country club. I was nineteen and a good golfer and I would go out at eight o'clock in the morning and play golf with my father and his businessmen friends. We'd get in at eleven or twelve o'clock and hit the men's clubhouse. We'd already had drinks at the fourteenth hole, and they were already halfway gone and they'd all be talking about their tax shelters and their big macho deals—sort of like lions preening in front of one another. I would leave early because I was still a kid. My mother would be back at the house with these guys' wives and they'd all be playing bridge. I'd end up being the bartender and I'd actually enjoy hanging out with these women because they were telling all these ridiculous stories about their husbands and what assholes they were—and I'd just left these men at the bar, these assholes. That women needed liberation never *occurred* to me. I knew perfectly well my mother even knew more about *business* than my father.

The thing I always loved dearly about my father was his being spaced-out, his philosophical bent. I just don't think he was well equipped for parenthood—probably not even for marriage. He should have been a philosopher, or a priest. For instance, he never had a checking account in his life. He used to come home with his paycheck and sign it over to my mother. She ran all the money in the family. There just was no question about who was in charge. At the time I didn't think of this as a sign of weakness in my father. I thought of it as a division of labor. She was much better at these things. My wife and I have a joint checking account—I deposit my paycheck and she deposits hers and then we feel free to spend the money. It's more like *our* money. With them, it was my mother's money, and my father got an allowance. She literally wrote the check for his commutation tickets and gave him X dollars a day.

During grammar school I always got crazy marks, depending on whether the nun liked me or not. I pretty much thought grammar school was a joke, because by the time I got there I could already read and write. But my marks were basically at the whim of the nuns. Even at the end I became valedictorian, though I didn't have the highest average, simply because I got into a very good private school.

At any rate, when I got to prep school I flunked every single subject except math on my first report card. I got the report card on Friday, and I knew if my parents saw it, it was going to blow my weekend, so I waited until Monday to show them. We were having dinner at my grandfather's house, and I told my mother and she said, "Wait till your father gets home!" He arrived about 8:30, after dinner was over, and my mother said, "Thomas, I want to see you for a minute." She took him into my grandfather's bedroom and showed him my report card. He said, "Well, what do you want *me* to do?" And she said, "Take him home and beat him." And that's exactly what he did. He put me in the car, took me home and beat me. It wasn't as if I got slapped in the face a couple times, this was a carefully thought out scourging. He took me into the bathroom and tied my hands to the towel rack. I was standing in the bathtub naked and he took an appliance cord, doubled it over leaving the two plugs on the end of it, and beat the living shit out of me. I still have welts on my body from it. I hated him for doing it. I hated him for following my mother's instructions. I felt betrayed by him, and also from that moment forward I realized that women had all the power. I almost felt like he and I were in the clutches of my mother, and that he was just as helpless a pawn as I was. Even my grandfather, who had heard my mother order my father to beat me, said, "Don't you dare lay a hand on that boy." So the next day I ran away from home and went to my grandfather's house, and he refused to give me back to them until they promised never to beat me again.

I remember my father telling me I'd gotten off easy with that beating, that he'd gotten worse beatings from his father—and I'm sure he did. I think this is just environmental training. Certainly one thing that stands out is that I am never, ever going to lay a hand on my daughter, no matter what.

Basically my father is a gentle man who likes harmony, even though he has his violent streak. He loves people and is very generous and compassionate.

There are so many values that my father has that I do appreciate. To this day the greatest joy I have is just to be able to sit there and space out in my head. Your consciousness and your intelligence give the greatest pleasure you can have, in many ways better than sex. It's inviolable.

On a visceral level I resent the fact that my father does not have balls. He's an emotional character; he's not a physical character and I see so much of this in myself. It's the thing I have to fight the most. I really like to be a nice person. But my father gets to the point where he lies, rather than make waves. He'll promise my mother he'll be home at 5:30 when he knows goddamn well it'll be 8:30. Then he'll call at 6:30 and say he got tied up a little, and he just keeps stringing people along like that. I don't think it's an inherent evil and maliciousness in him: it's a weakness. He was never able to face up to my mother. And she made it very difficult. "Look at Mr. Smith, he works in the stock market and gets home every day at 4:30 for martinis." Well, Mr. Smith happened to have inherited $50 million.

The thing is, my father still lives in this dream world of golf and country clubs because he was married to the princess on the hill whose father was worth $70 million.

When I got out of college I was in a dream world of my own. All through college I didn't think of majoring in marketing or business or anything like that. I really just concentrated on the classical education. My only exposure to business was as a laborer on a construction gang, which was sort of a "heroic" job for a college kid to have. I really had no notion of what I was going to do and waited for a month after graduation before I even started looking for a job. I started with IBM and quit after less than two weeks. The only work experience I was used to was being an iron worker on construction. I was totally confused. I just knew I was going to be taken care of. At this time we were living in our small perfect palace and I really had no notion that one had to go out and earn a living. So I split. I drove out to Berkeley and then came back and went to work as an iron worker. After about three weeks my father told me I ought to go into management. I did that for a year.

My mother was constantly saying, "Look at your father, he comes home at 8:30 at night covered with concrete and his suits are all disheveled. And look at Mr. Smith, he's in the stock market." So I quit the construction business and went into the stock market and did that for three years. And then I completely disowned both of them. Neither one of them was living the type of life I wanted. I didn't want that velvet coffin. My father's intellectual activity was crushed. Here was this guy who could have been a great philosopher sitting around talking to some asshole practical stockbroker who didn't understand what he was talking about. His growth was truncated twenty years ago or maybe even forty years ago. His life was a shambles, and my mother's life was a shambles because he wasn't a stockbroker: He was sort of this clumsy guy who was a little spaced out and wore funny clothes and was like the class clown of the country club.

I moved out of their house three months before my twenty-eighth birthday. I wanted to leave but I didn't know what to do because I was so used to the security blanket of the money and the club and having the maid make dinner. I still thought I had to wear pressed suits and starched shirts, but I knew there was something that was not quite right. Each of them wanted to mold me into something that I wasn't. My mother wanted to make me a perfect little hardball player at Morgan Stanley and my father wanted me to be a perfect hardball player who could hold his own with Thomas Aquinas. I could never please them no matter how good I was. I used to come home from these Junior League–type dances, and my mother would *quiz* me, and I'd have to give her a report card of who I'd danced with. Everything was a goddamn report card, and yet I was supposed to be living in a Fred Astaire movie and be gay and dashing.

My mother is the dominant influence in my life. She was a great castrater, and ever since then I have feared and respected women. My mother encouraged competition with my father. We used to have these little talks late at night because my father always went to bed early. We'd stay up until two or three in the morning and have these long heart-to-heart talks about how Daddy is an intellectual, and it's a great joy to you, but you have to be more practical. She'd get very touchy and say, "You're so smart and handsome and I love you so much and I just know with all your father's brains . . ." and she'd go on and on and on. I'm sitting there drinking wine and hanging out with Mom and getting these pep talks and—it's sort of like being an Oedipal victor, right? Everything she could not make her husband into, she laid onto me. She finally gave up on my father when he was forty-five or fifty and realized she was married to an absentminded space cadet who wasn't going to make the grade.

I feel my father has a great deal of resentment about these times with my mother. I don't think he likes being married to her—they're just caught up in the Catholic paradigm and now they've lived together for forty years. It's just too late now. In any event, my mother has made me feel manipulated by women, wary of women. I don't doubt their power for an instant.

My father and I broke off relations five years ago over a business deal. He cheated me out of some money and I haven't spoken to him since. I got heavily into alcohol after that, because the emotional pain was just too much. I couldn't understand how it happened. Somehow through thick and thin, I had always believed my father was loving. It wasn't as completely brutal as it sounds, but it was deliberate. My therapist says, "These people really brutalized you," and I say, "No, no, no, you don't understand, we had wonderful times, too." And he says, "Wake up. Everything

201

was wonderful and loving as long as you were their little automaton." But my emotional memories are not *all* bad. I still to this day believe my father really loves me. I guess he just loves himself more than he loves me. I think the reason he screwed me out of the money was that he wanted to show off for my mother. He ended up paying a worse price—the loss of me. Not only that, my mother knows in her heart of hearts that I put the deal together. I don't know what they really feel about it. They're so anesthetized by their country-club life.

We finally had a reunion at my daughter's christening. I realized that I had an obligation to her not to bring my personal hang-ups with my parents into her life. She has a right to know her grandparents. So I wrote to my parents and said, "I want to declare a truce, in the grand Christian tradition of festivals and feasts." But I told them I would never trust them again. My mother immediately responded and she arrived early for the christening. My father came three hours late. I had to actually seek him out and say, "Welcome." He walked in and was like some sort of caged, threatened animal.

Overall, I think my father was a dreadful failure. He just wasn't properly equipped given the context of the woman he married. His basic shortcoming is a failure of courage. He always thought of himself as one of fifteen mutts raised by an Irish immigrant.

My father would describe me as a failure, too, with the possible hope that I would be a late bloomer. One of the things he told me when I was little was that I was the only person he'd ever met who was smarter than him. Which is kind of a heavy thing. The greatest thing he's given me is the love of learning. I don't think I could make anything different about him without making his relationship with my mother different. I would have had him marry a different woman. They were just so ill-suited.

I wish he'd been stronger in standing up to my mother. I don't think he really meant to beat me. But his father beat him. My grandfather used to tell stories of violence. He worked his way over here shoveling coal into a boiler and arrived in New York with fifteen cents in his pocket. He went to work as a laborer on construction and had a very hard life. He ended up with fifteen kids so he must have had a lot of frustrations.

The first things that come to mind when I think of a father-son relationship are: adversary, mentor, frustration, love and hate. It's just all very contradictory: there are all those opposites present in our relationship. But he had his own battles to fight. I love him, but I guess because he could never express *his* love, I'll never be able to express mine. Well, maybe someday I will.

23

Dean and Tommy Colby,* two scruffy teenage brothers in T-shirts, blue jeans and bare feet, looked apprehensive and slightly bewildered. Both boys, sixteen and thirteen respectively, had been arrested for stealing bicycle parts, and on this steamy summer morning they sat in the waiting room of a juvenile detention center with their father and stepmother. After his parents' divorce, Dean was in the legal custody of his grandparents from the ages of six to eleven. For the past five years he has lived with his father. Tommy has only recently joined his brother. He has lived off and on with his mother and stepfather in the North, and in several foster homes. A towheaded boy with a disarmingly innocent face, Tommy is more open than his older brother, who is a rather reticent, cautious, and withdrawn boy. Travis Colby is the thirty-nine-year-old father of Dean and Tommy. He is an auto-parts mechanic.

Sometimes my boys and me get along good and sometimes we don't. Boys think they know a lot. I try to correct them; I try to explain to them things about the law they should know. They broke a law by stealing. I could have told them what would happen; I could have told them what juvenile hall would look like, but sometimes we don't communicate. They won't communicate with me and they won't communicate with my wife. They won't talk to us. I can see they've had some problems. When they lived with their mother . . . well, I feel they're holding something back. They don't want to discuss it with us. I just don't know what they're blocking from us. I heard about things that happened; I don't know if they're true, but I heard from other people they were locked out of the house in the hot sun all day. I was told they would have to pull vegetables out of people's gardens and eat them because they couldn't get any food. I heard people say they would have to sit in a swing all day long and not move. They won't talk to us about it. I know about it, but they're going to deny it. I think they don't want to go back to their past, to their bad experience.

We're trying to bring them up in a better environment than what they were in. My wife and I may be strict but we're trying to raise them up right. We're trying to keep them out of trouble and help them lead a straight life. We make them go to school, and if they want to mow yards, or something, I'll let them so they can make some money on the side. I even found them a job setting pins at a bowling alley. All my kids work. I got jobs for my stepson and my daughter, too. Dean likes to work on bicycles so I help him and try to explain what's got to be done. Tommy likes to work on lawn mowers. I'm very bad at that; but each kid likes to work on something and they like to ask my advice. If I have the knowledge I tell them what to do.

Are there things about myself I would change as a father? Well, I've lost my temper several times. I know there's a law against beating a child. I know that. I don't want to beat them but I have to discipline them somehow, some way. I've already tried restricting them. Right now they're restricted for one year because they violated a rule we made at home. I've tried putting them in a corner for an hour but it don't work. I've tried locking them in their room but it don't work. I've tried to spank them; it don't work. And I have to find some way of correcting my children to make them act normal instead of being bad. I have to make them respect their parents. When their parents say "do something," the children should do it now, right here. I have to tell them maybe two or three or four times.

The way I let them know I care about them is we sometimes take the whole family places to eat as a reward or something, you know. I ask them to clean up their rooms or something, and if they do a good job, I may give them a treat. I let them go get some ice cream or something. I sleep during the days and I work nights but when I'm up, I'm there. I do try to work with them and sometimes I even try to play with them. Once in a while they like to play basketball or catch. I try to play with them, but sometimes I can't do it because I have a bad leg.

My father I have not seen for many years. He's in a nursing home. He was hurt in a motorcycle accident and suffered brain damage. I have not been too close to my father at any time in my life. He's been in the hospital so long. I believe I was about six years old when it happened. All I had was my grandparents. They mostly raised me. I didn't want my way. I did what I was told. We got along good.

I can't say I ever cried about my father. But I never was close to my dad; that's just it, see. My daddy was a quiet man like I am. I'm a quiet person. He didn't talk much. When I was little, I know he took me places; we went fishing or camping. That was the only time I remember I was close to my dad. That's when the family was together. After he went into the hospital I didn't see him very much. I haven't seen him now for maybe fifteen years. He was a little bit standoffish and I'm a little bit that way with my sons. I try to work with them, but most times I can't do it. My hours I work, I just can't be with them.

No, I don't think it has anything to do with the trouble they're in. The reason they're in trouble is they all want bikes. I didn't know the parts were stolen. I was wondering why I was getting so many around the yard. All of a sudden I had four bicycles built. I couldn't figure out where they were coming from. Then somebody came to the house and said he recognized his bicycle parts. So I told the boys if they wanted a bicycle they had to save their money and buy their own. I told them they had to have a bill of sale to show me on that bike.

It's hard to answer what makes a good father. That's tough for me. The only thing I can see is a father should work with his children and try to help them—try to keep them in line. I show them that as long as they're under *my* roof they live the way I want them to live and stay out of trouble, obey our rules, and when I assign them a job I want to see that job done. That's what I think a father should do. If you don't work with them, then you're not interested in them. I have to see what's going on—I have to know what's going on—I have to work with them. I mean, I can't put it all on my wife's shoulders. I guess I'm not affectionate with them, but I can't say there's anything wrong with it.

Dean: My relationship with my father is all right. He'll sit down and talk to us when we do something bad. He's divorced from my mother and she lives in Illinois and we live with him. He's pretty strict; whenever we do something he punishes us. Either a restriction or a spanking. We don't get to see him too much because he works nights—he makes auto parts—and then he sleeps during the day. When we do see him, we usually go outside and play, or work together on jigsaw puzzles. The thing I like most about him is he treats us right when we're good. I'm on probation for stealing a bicycle. I took it because I needed the parts. He gets mad when I get in trouble. Sure, I'd rather make him happy—that would be by keeping out of trouble and doing what he says.

My brother and I work for our own money, so we have to buy things ourselves. We set up pins at a bowling alley after school.

If I had a son I guess I'd be pretty much like my dad: strict, but nice whenever he does things good. My dad's not affectionate, but I know he loves me just by the way he takes care of me. I don't see my friends' fathers too much. One of them has a pretty nice father; he's mean to him like my dad is to us when we're bad.

Tommy: When I watch TV with my father I like wrestling with him. He usually wins. I like him best when he plays around; sometimes we go out and play basketball. My mom's nicer than my dad. I don't get very much punishment from her. My stepdad is the one that spanks me. I live with my dad and my stepmom now. I just got down here from Illinois in March. I came 'cause I got in trouble, taking bikes and all. I was gonna sell them to get some money. I didn't have any money because my mom took it all. I had a paper route but she took the money every time I got paid. She didn't work and my stepdad didn't work. They were on disability. It made me kinda mad, but they did buy me something almost every month when they got a check. I'd rather live with my mom because I've been with her longer than my dad. I know her better. She wanted me to stay in Illinois but the court made me come here. Once I got in trouble I started going into foster homes and then I had a court hearing and they made me come down here and live with my father. It's not that bad living with him, but I'd still like to go back to my mother. Mothers stay around their kids more than fathers. The things that make a good father are treating your children right; and don't beat them, just correct them. I'll probably have children. I want boys and girls, both. I'd treat them the same. I'd correct them if they needed it, but otherwise I would just keep them and play around with them.

24

Mark David Chapman made international headlines when he shot and killed John Lennon. Shaken by the magnitude of his stunning destruction of a human life, this now convicted killer in his mid-twenties, closely guarded in a cold prison room, talked quietly, willingly and sadly about many experiences in his life. Against a background of the echoing sounds of laughing guards and clanking metal doors, he described his prevailing fantasy of murdering his father, of how he would have done it, and why.

I was going to break into his house, and get him in his room alone, and put a gun to him and tell him what I thought about him and what he had done to my mother, and that he was going to pay for it; and then I was going to blow his head off. First I'd just frighten him to death because he's not a very strong man, emotionally. I'd be holding on to him and say, "This is what you get, this is what is coming to you for what you've done to my mother and our family, and I hear you're scared to death that you're going to go to Hell, and this is it, Dad, you know, I'm not even going to give you another minute to live, I'm just going to blow you away and make you suffer; you're going to suffer in Hell for this," and then I was going to shoot him.

My father was never very emotional; I don't think I ever hugged my father. He never told me he loved me, and he never said he was sorry; he was one of those guys. And then my next memories were him beating up my mother; I'd wake up in the middle of the night and my mother would be screaming out my name, and it scared me . . . I mean, I'd jump out of bed and run in there and put up my fists, and, you know, make him go away; actually sometimes I think I'd . . . I'd even push him away. And I'd see her the next day—she'd have black eyes and bruises on her head and no telling what else because she didn't share it with me. But I remember distinctly waking up at least two or three times and hearing her scream my name out, and *that* is very traumatic and unsettling. We just never ever really got along. He smashed my head down in a plate of spaghetti one time, and he . . . I don't think he was a child beater but he did beat me sometimes, maybe three or four or five times.

He never showed any emotional love, just maybe if I needed money for school, he would give it. Mom always told me that my father couldn't show these kinds of things but he'd try to in other ways. You know, he was always home and he never drank and things like that, but I needed more than just a father who was responsible, morally—not morally, but maybe ethically—for his family. I needed more than that.

I needed emotional love and support. I never, ever got that and I think my life shows that I was always trying to get it with older males; my friends were always at least two years older, and I maybe looked upon them as father figures. I guess I just wanted my father's recognition. I wanted him to praise me every once in a while. The only thing he did for me was to try to bring me into his workshop and show me how things worked, and then I'd get bored with it because it was like a teacher. It wasn't like he was doing it for me, it was like he was doing it just because he felt he had to teach me these fundamentals of sawing and hammering and fixing things. But he'd get extremely frustrated and throw something, or cuss and walk out, you know. He was a great one for not being able to handle *any* circumstances contrary to what he thought was going to happen, I guess.

And I've got some of that in me, too. I burst into these rages and walk out and throw things; and I *hate* that part about me, that part that is my father. As I get older, I see more and more how I'm like my father and I don't want to see that part of me. I want to see me more like my mother, even though she's female. I learned more from her and got more experience from her than I did from my father.

My father's reaction [to the murder] was very blasé. I hadn't seen him in a while and I think he told me that he was disappointed; that's par for the course for my father's reaction. I have tried to block my father out as much as possible. I don't care about him; I've killed him in my mind already. I kill people in my mind that do something. The number one sin against me is to do something against me without cause. I've never done that to anyone in my entire life, done something to someone, evil and mean, without a cause. If someone comes up and I kick them and they kick back, there's still a chance that we can get along. But if someone comes up, particularly adults, and is nasty to me for no reason, because maybe I'm younger or something along those lines, it's all over, I mean, I won't even speak to them.

We're all murderers in a way because when you hate someone with your heart, you are in a sense murdering them, you won't let them live, you won't give them a chance, they're dead and buried, and there's nothing that can change your heart other than repentance and trying to turn yourself around, and that's what, in a sense, I did to a lot of people all these years because I felt that, that I didn't get a fair break from a lot of them, from most of them. And I try *so* hard to get along with people, and *try* to please them and *try* to get along, and *try* on their own level because I feel I'm on an adult level. And I've been through experiences, and maybe even more so than some of these adults, and yet they still wouldn't recognize me as an adult and as an equal and as someone to have an intelligent conversation with.

I think the relationship between a father and son is even more important than the relationship between a son and mother—

between the kids and the mother—because a father is the head of the household. He is the authority, he has the final decision; he is generally, although not so much anymore, but he is generally the one who supports the family financially. He should be the leader in that area, he should be a comforting kind of person and he should take leadership. My father took *no* leadership other than, you know, paperwork on the budget, and fix-it stuff if it broke around the house. That's about it. And making sure that we had food. We never went on vacation once, in our whole time. Every Thanksgiving we would go down to see my grandmother, but it really wasn't a vacation. But only one time do I remember that we ever did anything as a family. We went down to Florida and took in the sights—that was only for about four days. He was always so cheap, he was always so worried about money, so bothered about it. My mom said he could never handle money, never.

If I had a son I'd be very, very compassionate and loving, and I would give him as much love as my wife, maybe more so. Physically, I would show it . . . I would hug and kiss him—well, I'd kiss him until he was a certain age—and I'd just let him know that he could come to me to talk about anything, and that I would support him in anything, and hold him, and let him know that I was the father, that I was the male, I was the head of the family *but* I was also a human being and that he could trust me and come to me at any age and get advice, and get *love;* and tell him that I loved him and when I made a mistake in front of him, tell him, "Son, I'm sorry, I know I'm your father and you think a lot of me but I am a human being also and I just made a mistake; if you'll forgive me, we'll just go on from here." Those are the things I would tell my son.

25

Sag Harbor, Long Island, a village in the Hamptons that is best known as the summer playground for New York journalists, has been the lifelong home of thirty-year-old Dennis Boyle, a house painter and handyman with the trusting good nature of the true "local." Though Mr. Boyle was only months old when his father died, he nonetheless has a sharp and solid image of the man he never knew.

Everything I know about my father has come from his friends, my mother, and my brothers and sisters. I was the youngest child of six children, only fifteen months old when he died at age forty-eight. The joke I always told is that my father looked at me and said, "That's enough! Fifteen months is enough! I'm getting outta here before he walks!"

Genetically you're always influenced by both parents, and I often think about the traits I have that might reflect his. My father was compassionate toward other people. He was a sucker—and I don't mean that in a bad sense—for helping people. When they first built the Christmas nativity scene down in Sag Harbor, he lent a hand. He helped youth organizations, and if someone asked him to lend a hand, he'd be right there. That's a fault I have. Most times I take care of everybody else before I take care of myself, and sometimes I have to stop and put things in perspective. But I think it's in the genes. I have a tendency to always think of the good things even though I know there are some bad ones, too. My father used to go out and have a few beers and sometimes would drink to excess, so I try to keep an eye on my alcohol. If I've been drinking for two or three days, I'll stop automatically on the fourth day. Alcoholism runs in the family, and I feel it can affect relationships with other people. So I try to moderate it, based a lot on what I've heard of my father.

When I was a kid I used to cry if my mother was sick, or every once in a while I would just cry thinking, "What happens if I lose my mother? Where am I going to be?" We're a pretty tight family, and I had the benefit of having my brothers and sisters take care of me as well, because there was so much difference in age; I was a change-of-life child, born when my mother was forty-four. But I didn't want to end up being a burden to everyone else, just like my mother didn't want to be a burden to my older brother Jerry. He was seventeen when my father died. My father was a butcher, and my brother was learning to be a butcher at the time of his death. Jerry quit school and became a manager of a shop, and ironically ended up managing the shop my father started. He supported the family, and to this day he sends my mother $20 a week.

I considered Jerry something of a replica of my father in that he had the same traits and similar diversions, so in a way he represented my father. But Jerry didn't really become a father image to me. He's always been my brother—a brother who's done a lot for me. When I was younger there were things everybody would go through like Cub Scouts, and the fathers would be present for ceremonies and functions. That made me a little envious of my friends. It was very important for me to get my brother to go.

My father's death was explained to me in a religious way. God was part of the household, and I was told my father had gone to Heaven. It was always to Heaven. I don't know if he went to Heaven or not! But we accepted that; we accepted the loss because there was no other way to deal with it at that time. So I guess I didn't really feel envious of other boys as much as I felt cheated. I would have liked to experience having my father there for things like basketball, track, dinners.

I sometimes lecture friends who despise their parents. I tell them don't hate them, give it a shot and try to communicate a little better. At least there's somebody there you can talk to who won't be there some day. I didn't have my father all through my life, and I wish I'd had that chance they're abusing.

It's difficult for me to say what might have been because I grew up during the sixties and seventies in an independent time—independence of thought, questioning of parents. I rebelled against my mother, but I never wanted to *hurt* her. My mother's biggest thing was a guilt trip: "You're killing me, Dennis! You're gonna kill me!" All that nonconforming trendy stuff of the sixties like long hair would probably have been tough for my father, who grew up in a totally different era. Jerry and I used to have real heavy arguments. He'd say, "Shape up or ship out." My father was not a physically abusive person, but he'd probably have been angry over the way I acted. I think if he hadn't died, I'd still be as close to my mother but not so protective. Maybe my decision about where I went to college would have been different, too. I probably would have tried for U.C.L.A. or some other powerhouse rather than staying in the East. I had a track scholarship, you see, but I didn't feel I should go too far away from my mother.

I never felt any bitterness about my father's death. The first time I took a friend to his gravesite on the North Shore, I cried. That was last summer, and it was the first time I'd cried about him passing away since I was a little kid. It's because I have a daughter now, a family, and I wish my father could have seen her. And I'd brought a friend and I wish he could have seen *him*. Those things are special, and I would have liked to share them with my father.

223

26

Michael Carter* is a clean-cut, tweedy, usually pensive research scientist from Washington, D.C. He is a bachelor in his mid-thirties.

In my thirty-five years, I probably have known my real father less than six months. By that I mean I've actually been in his physical presence only that much. I can't even remember how old I was when my parents divorced. I was too young. After that he was out of my life—so this disqualifies me completely, doesn't it? I don't remember anything about my father during my early years. He was in the service until the 1970s. He was fighting a war in the Pacific and then he was—well, I don't know *where* he was. I can't answer much about him because I don't really know anything. He might might be a member of the Mickey Mouse Club, for all I know, or one of Mao Tse-tung's guerrilla leaders.

The few months that I *have* spent with my father were not initiated by him. They were initiated by me out of curiosity—no, curiosity is the wrong word—out of a desire to know him. If my curiosity had been stimulated, those few months would have turned into a longer period of time, because things would have blossomed.

Things *didn't* blossom because—well, I don't want to say anything bad, because I don't know him. Our relationship is at arm's length, it's third person. He's another man, he's like an uncle more than a father. In fact, he's more like a stepuncle. When I have gone to his house I've found him a very proper and pleasant man, but he's never had children in his life and therefore he doesn't respond to me or to young people in a fatherly way.

Yet I can remember the few times I was with him he would ask me somewhat ridiculous questions and I would give him very concise, articulate and philosophical answers. He'd ask why do young men these days wear long hair? Why are they demonstrating at Berkeley? Why did they kidnap Patty Hearst? And my answers—well, I didn't answer the questions per se, but I would explain that generation and he would say, "Now that's a good answer."

I guess you could say there's very little emotion attached to our relationship. It's just a man-to-man type thing, it's not a father-son thing. The only *love* I feel is when I hear he's had an ailment. He's slightly concerned because his classmates have been dying off, and when we did get together one of the first things he'd say was, "Mr. Jack X died last week, and, boy, I'm really feeling it, you know." I don't even know who Mr. Jack X *was*. So my love toward my father would only be because this is my blood father and he *is* getting older.

A natural incident encouraged my wanting to get to know my father. I was in the United States Army. I went through officer candidate school while he was still an active air force colonel. The laws of the U.S. military say that a field-grade officer or better can do the swearing in of new lieutenants. I was about to be sworn in, so I called him up. I'm sure he was proud that his son was graduating from officer candidate school. I asked him if he would consider doing the swearing in, and so he and my mother and my sister were all present. I was sworn in by him and a year later went to Viet Nam. Going to Viet Nam you go through San Francisco, which is where he was living. I saw him going over, and I corresponded with him and saw him coming back. A couple years after that my interest in my father started to grow. Whenever I had an opportunity to go to San Francisco I would pursue it so I could visit with him. I found it interesting to talk with him because he seemed to be so fascinated by the society he was living in. He was not really tuned in to it, having been in the air force all his life. The military is certainly a society all on its own that is quite divorced from the society of the civilian world—the Patty Hearsts, the stock market transactions, the commercial business, the homosexuals in San Francisco. So my interest in being with him has only been perpetrated on those short weekends. He's like a stepuncle, a remote friend. There are no father-son feelings.

I was with my stepfather from the age of five to fifteen, but that was twenty years ago. And in those twenty years he has been virtually completely absent. My pursuits in establishing a father-son relationship have been directed toward Mr. Carter, my real father. Therefore, though my stepfather served as a father image in those formative years, he's not been like a father to me since. So we're back again to base one. I don't relate to either one of them.

My mother's love was always there and it's real. I can't say that it was a replacement for the love of my absent father. My mother is my family, and my father and my stepfather . . . they weren't there. I say that, but I don't mean that I was deprived of anything. When I was living with my stepfather I was at an age where I associated him with father, and I certainly did love him. I called him by his first name but I also called him Father, I think. I did not call him Dad, though.

The closest moment between my real father and me was when I, as a second lieutenant departing for Viet Nam, spent a week with him before going. We didn't talk about it very much. I put on my uniform and he drove me out to Travis Air Force Base. While we were crossing the Golden Gate Bridge, he said something to me that I remembered many a time while I was in Viet Nam. And I remember it to this day with such vividness that I bring it up. We were driving across the bridge in his old Dodge automobile and he said, "Twenty-five years ago *my* father drove me across this bridge to go fight a war in the Pacific. Here I am driving *you* across this bridge to go fight a war in the Pacific. God forbid you ever have to drive *your* son across this bridge to go fight still another war." I thought about it because it was a very profound historical thought. At that moment it didn't mean a thing to me, but later I remembered it many times. And I remember it not with respect to the relationship between a father and son but as a fascinating line about the world we live in.

My father never calls me. I always call him. He never writes. I write him. But I like him the way he is—which is Uncle Bud. Or rather, I accept him the way he is. I would love to change him to where when I arrive he would take three days off from whatever he's doing and say, "Come on! Let's go up to Yosemite." Or, "Let's go up to Nevada and gamble. Let's smoke cigars and play poker." You know, do *something* that . . . but he's not like that. And I know that now. And for me to expect him to change, or try to make him change and fit a different mold—it won't happen. He's a retired colonel in the air force, and he treats me with the greatest and highest respect. And he probably would *like* to treat me a little more like a son but to do so he would have to go back thirty years.

I call him once every three months. I see him once every four months maybe for a week. I think what has brought us together is that several years ago I gave him a little automobile. And this year his second automobile was fading and dying so I gave him another automobile. So he now has my Mustang convertible, and he *loves* it. He hasn't had the roof up on that car for two years. So I call him and I say, "How's the Mustang?" And he'll talk to me for twenty minutes telling me how much he likes that Mustang. He likes talking to me about it because he knows it came from *me*.

This interview must seem awfully dry. When you say father-son relationship I say, excuse me, what relationship? When I was living with my stepfather and I was just a young man, the classic thing was the son out hunting and fishing with the father. When I was learning to use a shotgun or rifle, my stepfather had this great chauffeur named Leslie, and *Leslie* taught me how to shoot and fish. I went with *him*.

Okay, this has *got* to have affected my personality and how I react with other men and women of my own age. Probably especially women, but that comes from my mother filling so much of my life. I find the men I get along with, I get along with wonderfully. We have respect and admiration for each other. We've earned each other's friendship. The women? I'm not married and that might . . . that might be it. And maybe I just haven't thought about it enough. Maybe I *should* think about it but I'm not worried or upset or lost. Marriage is such a difficult institution.

I have a lot of male friends. I'm a jock, an athlete. I *have* looked to older men as mentors. Every now and then I'll feel a little bit lonely in the professional world I'm in, and I need a strong intelligent person in the commercial world who is wiser than me and whom I can look up to. I've found that in a couple of people. These are gentlemen my father's age.

I call my father every three months because I know he appreciates my company. It is a very narrow world he lives in. He is married to a woman who is not his intellectual companion, and he lives in a society that he cannot intellectually comprehend because of all those years in the military. But he is a man who has basic curiosities about the world that he was a defender of—about the draft, about the people in college, about the demonstrations, about the new president—and I don't think he has any intellectual springboards. You try living a life like that—my father has done it for fifteen years now. It begins to haunt you. You *need* someone to talk to. Whenever I do call him he just talks and talks and asks questions.

The most demonstrative period of our relationship was when I graduated from OCS and became an officer in the United States military. He got on an airplane and flew out there and swore me in and shook my hand and he had the smile of the proud father. That gave me a sense of family that I guess I've never felt. My mother was there proud of me too, but they were not jointly proud of me, they were individually proud of me. So I had to respond to my father on one side and my mother on the other—it wasn't competition but there is no *family*. But maybe it's like I was fortunate enough to have *two* families.

I occasionally see habits in me that I think came from him: being quiet, going off by myself. I regret to announce that I am not so proud of those habits. My mother and my sister are outgoing, industrious, socially gregarious, and they put a lot into everyday life. My father is a reserved, proud, introverted man. I find myself somewhat like that, and I sometimes wish I had more of the gaiety of the female side.

I probably have a few misconceptions about the male-female roles. My interpretation of a man may be a little classic and outdated: the strong man, the hunter, the athlete. This older, traditional concept of a man has not been dispelled by having a father present in whom I can see faults. So therefore to me men are always the leaders. That's rather chauvinistic, I'm afraid. The only father I've seen is a distant father: I never see the petty weaknesses, the daily scratching and itching and brushing of teeth like the rest of us. So my interpretation of manhood is based on things I've read or heard rather than on things I've experienced—except in myself. I just won't show my weaknesses because men aren't supposed to have them.

If I were to have a son, I'm sure I wouldn't be a very close father the first several years. I'm just not that close to small children, but they wouldn't be small forever. I want children for egotistical reasons. I don't have any genetic problems, I'm a good provider, I could rear them intelligently—I think I could be a very good father. I don't know, though, if I can exactly answer what makes a good father. I mean, the father is a complement to the mother and

I'd have to define the two characters together as parents—and here I am saying this having *not* come from that environment. I don't look at the mother as the housewife or maid of the family, not at all, but the father has got to be the strong and rational one.

Emotional people do not make good parents. You should express your love to a certain degree, but too much is not good. That means responding to every whine and every holler—I mean, there's got to be discipline. Discipline comes from allowing love in rational proportions. Imagine the figure of a Maltese cross. On the top you've got rational, on the bottom you've got emotional—you can almost call them opposing forces. On the left hand side you've got instinct; on the right, intelligence or intellect. And the character is always moving back and forth and around the Maltese cross on these four axes. The man in society is basically a little more toward the rational side than he is toward the emotional side, and the woman a little more toward the emotional side than the rational. I'm not exactly sure about these things, though, because I'm not familiar with the rearing of children and male-female relationships within a marriage.

The first year of childhood is mostly diapers and crying and bottles. I think in that period I would like to support my *wife,* not the child. I would want *her* to support the child. When my first niece was born and she was happy in her mother's arms and my sister would say, "Here, don't you want to hold her?" I would say, "No, no, not right now." When the child starts thinking, when it has its first thoughts that were planted, that were sort of motivated, that's when I become fascinated.

Because my relationship with my father is so shallow—or so undeveloped—you're getting it all. I can sum up in twenty minutes of tape or chitchat the entire relationship. What I have just gone over pretty much sums up most of the thoughts I have had about my father, and that's unfortunate. Because if you sat down with someone who'd lived with his father for thirty-five years you would get an entirely different thing.

27

Mike Douglas—admired by millions who have viewed his talk show daily for almost twenty years—spoke seriously about his frustrations, his successes and his father, amid the clatter of dishes and echoing voices in an almost empty Hollywood restaurant during a very late afternoon lunch.

I loved my dad dearly but I never felt the same love in return. He was not a demonstrative guy. He was a real tough, professional Irishman, a tough disciplinarian. He was kind of a part-time father. My older brother was really the one who guided me through the formative years because Dad was a gambler and he didn't spend all that much time with the kids. He was there, but he was either reading or sleeping. He'd drink occasionally, and it's difficult to communicate with people when they're drinking unless you're drinking, too. So it was not what I'd call a warm, fifty-fifty relationship.

Even on vacation when I wanted to go fishing with him, he'd get up and go with the guys and I would wind up with an uncle or my brother or grandfather—when I really wanted to go with my dad because he was such fun. He had a great sense of humor; he was so witty. I wanted to be around him. I wanted to be like him in the worst way. I just wanted to do everything he did. I loved him so dearly . . . and I don't think he ever realized it. If he'd realized it—it still wouldn't have been a warm relationship, because he wasn't the kind of guy to put his arm around you. I guess it's an Irish trait—they're tough.

He stressed education first, but he also said never take anything from anybody. Never take, as he put it, bullshit, and he made us all fight. I didn't really want to. It's not my nature, but I thought, to make him happy, I'll do it. I became very good at it. I wanted to impress him. I thought, If fighting impresses him, then I'll do it, I'll beat everybody. And I got to the point where I looked for fights as a teenager. I wanted to make him so proud, and it never entered my mind that I could be hurt or disfigured or put out of business for life.

I remember one time I was walking down the street with my mother and dad and there was a group of guys playing baseball. Dad never forgot this. I think this was when I made him the proudest of me. I was dressed in a really nice outfit, a little bit flashy. I was a band singer, and I thought I was hot stuff. These guys were shouting things at me: "There goes a sissy with his mom and dad." There were about five of them. I remember walking across the street, all alone, with my mother standing there watching. I said, "I'm gonna take you all one at a time." One of them was a Golden Gloves champion, and when I got to him he said, "I can't fight you. I don't have my mouthpiece." I had already taken care of two of them. I said, "I don't have a mouthpiece either." He wouldn't fight and they called it off. Dad talked about that until he breathed his last breath, he was so proud of me.

I'd like my father to have taken me more places with him, perhaps on a couple of fishing trips, a hunting trip. I remember one time he came home on a Saturday feeling a little good. He worked half a day on Saturday which really meant getting together with the guys and having a couple of beers. Some neighbor of ours had a boy about my age who was flying a kite, and I must have had a look in my eye that said, "Gosh, I wish I had a kite." Only because he was under the influence of the sauce he said, "Would you like a kite?" He became wonderful when he drank beer, more demonstrative, more loving, more caring, for some reason. When he drank hard liquor he was violent, I mean *violent*. Anyway, he took me to a store and bought a kite and one ball of string. The other kid had more string and his kite was way out beyond mine and Dad said, "Ours looks kind of tacky compared to his, go buy more string." I ran as fast as my legs would carry me and bought another ball of string. I sat down and let that out all the way, and it became a contest. Later I found out that my dad didn't like this neighbor. He didn't buy the kite to please me, he wanted to top that neighbor. I never forgot that.

Dad solicited freight for a railroad and it meant he could leave the office and be on his own, which was not good. His boss told me that my dad could sell horse manure for wild honey. He was the best salesman ever. He charmed people right out of their shoes. He was great with the jokes. Everybody loved him. When he retired, I'd never seen an affair like that. Everyone came to me and said, "He's my best friend." So he was wonderful to other people, but I guess it wore him out doing that, and he didn't have anything left when he got home.

I remember, in Catholic schools they used to rank students on report cards. If you were the smartest, it said rank one, if you were second, rank two, and so on. There were forty-two people in my class. I brought home my report card and he looked at the bottom and said, "What does this mean, rank two?" I said, "I'm the second smartest person in the class." You know what he said? "Why aren't you number one?" You know what I was the next month? Twenty-second. He took it all out of me.

I wasn't his favorite. Everything I heard was about my older brother—"You know what Bob did?" Bob, Bob, Bob. It got to the point where it began to prey on my mind, so I was out to prove something. When Ella Fitzgerald turns to me and says, "Why don't you sing more on the show, you sing great,"—you know what that means to me? I don't want to be just anyone. I want to be the best. That was my father's favorite expression: The Best. Those two words. It was only toward the very end that he admitted that what I did was kinda special.

When he was living in Florida he called me up one day and said, "Have you seen Jim Bishop's column?" I said, "No, I haven't. What does it say?" He said, "It says you make two million dollars a year." And without hesitation I said, "That's right." And there was absolute silence. He could not *conceive* of this. That call was the longest call I had gotten from him in ages. He said, "Is that more than Carson makes?" And I said, "Yes." At the time it was. That was all he wanted to know: was that more than Carson makes.

I took care of him when he got older, but the only time I felt any resentment from him for being so dependent on me was when he became very ill right before he died. He said, "I'm gonna cash in my chips." He was tough, remember, like nobody else in the world. I said, "This isn't *my* dad talking." He said, "I'm such a burden on you," and his voice broke when he said it. He said, "This is it, I'm going into the hospital." And about three weeks from that phone call he died.

He told me he loved me the day before he died, but I had to initiate it. I leaned over and said, "I love you and you're going to be fine." And he repeated my words. He told me he loved me, too.

If I had a son, I would embarrass him, I would love him so much. I'm doing it to my grandson—hugging and grabbing him all the time. My grandchildren are so wonderful and beautiful. And they're part of *me*.

28

Christopher Binns'* characteristic puckish wit and frolic-
some nature were nowhere evident in the solemn portrait he
presented of his father, a retired salesman in Indiana. Mr.
Binns is a twenty-nine-year-old homosexual living in Los
Angeles.

I would say my relationship with my father is very distant, at best. He was a first-generation German-American, from a very European family, so I was brought up with the idea of the father going to work and the mother staying at home. There was very little interaction. I saw him briefly in the evening and occasionally in the morning, but as far as any sort of closeness, it didn't really exist. He was not particularly affectionate. I think I craved it when I was younger, but I built up defense mechanisms and channeled my energies in other directions. I became very active in school.

I was definitely closer to my mother because she was always there. Whenever I needed something, physical or emotional, she was there. My father *wasn't* there. I don't think it was a matter of his not loving me—he just wasn't particularly *interested* in me. He wasn't capable of having a relationship with another human being.

I'm the eldest of four children. There are two boys and two girls, and he's closer to my brother. My brother is a very good athlete, and my father was, too—he was a champion golfer—so they were able to relate on that level. I became an athlete for a while, but he still wasn't interested in me. So it was like Catch-22.

I was not at all close to my brother when we were growing up. We were constantly at each other's throats. It was rivalry, sure. Oh, definitely I was jealous of his being a little closer to my father. When I was five years old I got run over by a car. Before that I remember being real active, real athletic, always outside playing. After that I had to be still and quiet. I was afraid to do anything involving movement. During this time my brother was turning into a super athlete. My father noticed the difference and he reacted toward me differently from then on. My brother had a camaraderie with him that I just never had. My father touched him more, you know, hugged him more. I was upset that I didn't have that. I tried to do special things to get his attention—overachievement, for one. I was very good in music and art and I was a champion swimmer. My brother didn't know how to swim at all, so that was my ace in the hole. But by that time it didn't make any difference to my father. I mean, he was proud of me in his own way, but he was also a little embarrassed that I was involved in music and art rather than baseball or football. He knew what boys were supposed to be like. To him, playing baseball and football were what you were meant to do. And I was not like that at all. He was very cautious of me—to this day he still is.

Possibly my relationship with my father had something to do with the way I developed sexually, but I also think it's more physiology than environment. I was about seven when I really became attracted to males. I did not have sexual relationships, I was just fascinated with a boy in sixth grade. He was a real strong athlete, and he had the best flattop in school. I would wake up in the morning and draw pictures of him playing baseball. I was totally obsessed. When I got older I was attracted to athletes in high school.

I wish my father had been a little warmer and more interested in me. I wish he had been somebody who participated more in family life. My mother was a passive-aggressive type—not domineering. My father was a clothing salesman and he was usually drunk. He never ate meals with us. He would just come in and sit in a chair by himself. My parents have recently separated, so things have changed a little. He's in a program now to get over his alcoholism. He has a lot of problems to deal with before he can relate to other people. He has to find out who he is, because he's been in a stupor for thirty-five years. That's a long time. All of a sudden you wake up and the rest of the world and your family have gone beyond you. He tries now to be nice to me. But there's a lot of damage that's been done, and I'm not willing yet to say let bygones be bygones. He tore down a lot of self-esteem in all of us. When I was a child I had terrible guilt feelings about my father drinking. My first reaction was that it was my fault. Then I got very angry. Then I felt, I can't do this and I can't do that, because I'm not worthy. It took a long time to get over that and to realize I was my own person, that I was what I made of myself.

You know, I remember when my father was young he was very handsome. He looked like a movie star of the thirties and forties, like Errol Flynn. He was a great golfer and should have been a professional, except he didn't have the money. When I was a little boy I felt I couldn't live up to this image of him. I *knew* I couldn't live up to what he had been. I wanted to at the time, but my expectations finally changed until one day I no longer wanted it.

Conclusion

In the course of conducting the preceding interviews, I found that, in the main, fathers and sons either have or crave loving relationships. It is obvious that men *want* to be more nurturant, but stereotypes have a way of persisting. Too often the father's role has been relegated to that of the "heavy"—the stern disciplinarian who doles out punishment and little more. How many times have children been told, "Wait until your father gets home!" If the father is seen as an aloof authoritative figure without nurturant qualities, the result may be rebelliousness. A son's rebellion is very often simply a way of striking out at the unyielding father. I have my doubts as to whether adolescent rebellion is, in fact, a universal phenomenon. Often when adolescents are thought to be rebelling, they are really establishing their own individuality. In order to do so, they may try out new things as a way of taking on different roles. A loving, approving parent who is able to say, "I don't approve of that," but still respects the child's individuality, is not likely to inspire rebellion. On the other hand, a parent who says, "You do it my way or else!" could well end up with a defiant child.

The acceptance of a son's individuality is crucial to his sense of identity. We live in a society that urges us to be individuals, and yet parents sometimes tend to force their children to conform to certain standards. I believe, however, that we're beginning to see a greater acceptance of individuality, particularly among younger fathers who regard their sons as separate beings, and not simply chips off the old blocks, mirror images that affirm their own identity. The establishment of individuality must start very early in a child's life, and fathers play no small role in the process. While *both* parents must be consistent in setting limits, in drawing clear-cut boundaries for behavior, at the same time they must be willing to allow the child his uniqueness. Along with that is the need for responsiveness. What can be more excruciating for a child than a lack of emotional response from his parents?

Older men tended to have acted more in accordance with what was, in their day, appropriate to the father role, and in the way their own fathers acted: they were generally neither physically demonstrative nor actively involved in the day-to-day rearing of their sons. They often ruefully acknowledged that fact. "My relationship with my father was a much more distant one than with my children," reflected Gerard Piel, publisher of *Scientific American.* "He took an enormous interest in his kids, but he did it in kind of a secondary, ricochet way. There were four boys in the family and he became very much involved in the Boy Scouts, but he took it on a large, institutional basis, writing elaborate constitutions and marvelous sorts of rituals. It was very much through this sort of screen that he related to us. He was more verbally and histrionically demonstrative than physically. There was no horseplay. He wouldn't have *dreamed* of horseplay. I think I was closer to my children. There was lots of horseplay, and touch football and wrestling. But in the early years of their lives, I was very much involved in my career, working in a competitive environment at

Time Inc. I've been a workaholic ever since I can remember. So my days with my children were Saturdays and Sundays, and those were always reserved for some kind of adventure—sledding, museums, going to the country, going fishing. My son Jonathan is a much better father than I was—affectionate, concerned, attentive. I think he gives his kids more time and more love than I gave mine."

Younger fathers appear to me to represent a generation in transition. There is a marked reaction to what they perceive as their fathers' aloofness, to the lack of demonstrative affection or participation in their rearing. These younger fathers are making conscious, usually concerted efforts, to establish emotional and physical closeness with *their* sons and to spend as much time with them as possible. In short, they are attempting to correct what they regard as the mistakes of the past. What was striking in the interviews was the intensity with which they verbalized their feelings about subjects that would have once been, if not outright taboo, at least embarrassing. They spoke openly about affection and tenderness. Thirty-two-year-old Jeff Schwartz, for instance: "My father and I have always been very physically affectionate. To this day I still kiss him. I'll do it after a long absence, or if something has made me happy, or I'll just look at him and say, 'Hey, I love you, Dad.' And I'll give him a hug without any feeling of embarrassment. I am aware that this is not the norm, but I do not believe there is anything wrong with a man showing his affection. As a matter of fact, it's healthy. I'd say compared with my male friends, I'm more the exception than the rule. They're more macho. They're all on ego trips, they have a lot of hang-ups, they're uncomfortable with themselves. If my father had been aloof and unaffectionate, I'd most definitely be different today. His warmth and kindness helped me develop in my own way. It allowed me the open-mindedness to examine things and the freedom to be what I want."

A forty-four-year-old unmarried journalist, remembered that his father "was not affectionate, but one of the warmest memories I have is sitting in his lap and having him read the Sunday comics to me, and feeling his Sunday morning whiskers. If I had a son, I'd probably be a little bit more physical with him, and I guess that's what I would have changed in my relationship with my father: I'd have had *him* be a little more physical with *me.*" Not one male interviewed wished his father had been *less* demonstrative, and no one said, "My father was demonstrative, but I won't be that way with *my* son." They also spoke consistently of the necessity for fathers to spend time with sons. The majority stressed that they would like to spend—or would like to have spent—more time together.

According to Ahmet Temel, "It's very important to spend time with a child. When I was growing up, my father and I would take long walks together, and he would take me to his office once in a while. I didn't like his office, but it was a very fine feeling to be there." And Bill Mueller, thirteen, describing what it means to him to be with his father, says: "I don't see my father very much. Well, I see him on weekends, but he works a lot and sometimes he's in Japan for a month. When he comes home from work we eat and then he usually stays in his room and watches TV or works on papers. It's not that great like this, because when we don't see each other, we don't share our opinions or stuff like that. I'd like to be with him a lot more. When he's home at night watching TV, I'll walk in and out all the time just to see how he's doing. If he calls me in for something, I'll go running. He took me on my first hunting trip this weekend. Just this morning, when we were sitting in a duck blind by ourselves, where it was cold and the wind was blowing and there was no roof, just sitting there looking around, trying to be quiet—that was one of the best times I've had with him. We talked a little bit about a movie I saw and he was asking me how it ended, and we just talked about things while we waited. I like being alone with him. It makes you feel really close."

Children not only need time, they need to feel there is

something special, something exclusive about the attention they receive from their fathers.

A father's absence may well cause the son to turn more to his mother, thus raising the question of whether or not it is the time factor that has reinforced the general notion of the mother as the more nurturant parent. Take the case of the seven-year-old who said of his father: "I like him because he spends more time with me than my mother. . . . It feels like my father almost takes care of me more than my mother."

Even though Freud dealt with the import of the father's presence in the son's life, only recently has attention been truly focused on the role of the father in the development of the child's personality. Studies indicate, for example, that males without fathers are more likely to show poor academic performance and to have more problems with confused gender identity. Even a father who is present in the family but who spends little time with his children may contribute to similar developmental problems, albeit to a lesser degree. I would venture the theory that male homosexuality is more a function of thwarted affectional ties with the father than it is a result of the more commonly held notion of the domineering, manipulative mother.

Research conducted with young children whose fathers were in the service during World War II revealed that there was more "feminine orientation" among boys whose fathers were absent during the children's infancy compared to those whose fathers were at home—and this feminization continued even after the father's return.

Mrs. Travis Colby, stepmother of Dean and Tommy Colby, the delinquent brothers arrested for stealing bicycles, offered her point of view on the relationship between the boys and their father, which serves as a further indication: "I get the impression the boys never had any time with their father until we got married. They might resent me, I don't know, because I tend to push them back

251

on him so they'll get closer together. They've never been that close—they're still not that close. The younger one is more playful because he's got that type personality. The older one is like his father—very standoffish, very much to himself.

"Their father really hasn't spent too much time with them. When we first got married, he was working six days a week—he *still* works six days a week, but I told him that I noticed when I was single and raising my own son I paid a lot of attention to him; he was the only one around me. I noticed that my husband's sons didn't act like my son. Really I guess I sort of compared them, and I don't know if that's wrong or right. You know how small kids will come and get in bed with adults? Well, my son will be twelve years old and he still comes and gets in bed with me in the morning. Well, my husband's sons have never done that. That's one of the things I've observed. There's no real affection. I think affection is necessary, but it's so hard to teach someone who never had it. They sort of reject it, because they think it's strange or weird or something. Maybe by the time they're thirty years old they'll realize it's okay. Maybe they'll be different if they have kids. I hope so."

Christopher Binns, the twenty-nine-year-old homosexual, described his relationship with his father as "distant, at best. There was very little interaction. I saw him briefly in the evening and occasionally in the morning, but as far as any sort of closeness, it didn't really exist. I was closer to my mother because she was always there. My father *wasn't* there. I don't think it was a matter of his not loving me—he just wasn't particularly *interested* in me. He wasn't capable of having a relationship with another human being."

Other studies show a definite relationship between antisocial behavior in boys and the absence of an adequate male figure to identify with during childhood. The father in these cases may have been literally absent, or he may have been present but unresponsive. Over and over again such disturbances in the father-son relationship prove to be associated with juvenile delinquency and crime. I think there is a need for a child to have contact with the father to establish a standard of right and wrong. If the contact is not there, then the child is at risk of developing a defective conscience and identity. My own clinical experience tells me that most delinquent acts in some way are a retaliation against an authority figure for neglect. Mark Chapman, John Lennon's assassin, is an example of a male whose father was there, but was emotionally unresponsive.

Moreover, the intensity of a young boy's "masculine interests" depends a great deal on the image he has of his father. The more masculine boys see their fathers as more powerful *and* more nurturant. This utterly demolishes the idea that if you want a manly son, you must be a tough, aggressive, manly father. On the contrary: you also have to be tender. "When my mom comes and kisses me good night," said one young boy, "I tell her to go get my dad, and he comes to kiss me, too. It doesn't make you feel like a sissy. It makes you feel secure all the time."

There is still, alas, the residue of the old macho notion that the expression of tenderness is not masculine. I profess the idea that such a feeling may be more nearly a compensation for a weak identity. A male with a weak identity would be more inclined to reject tenderness simply because it is threatening. If a male feels inadequate, he may overcompensate with macho behavior. Machismo is not so much a *reflection* of masculinity as it is a reaction to a male's *feeling* about masculinity.

But many of those interviewed felt that what makes a good father is essentially what makes a good mother: a caring, loving, responsive, protective, *nurturant* person. Nurturing means not only loving, but answering a child's needs—including his need to be fed, diapered and cuddled.

While it is clear that there's a need for the presence of the father, knowing he is *psychologically* there seemed to compensate, in a sense, for the lack of time he spent with his son. "I knew that if I needed my father he was there," remembered *Town & Country* publisher David McCann. "I could always lean on him. That in itself is an expression of love."

Conversely, one might ask, "If the father is physically there but psychologically absent, does that suffice?" The answer is no, it doesn't. Having the father present but emotionally unresponsive may be an even *greater* frustration. One of the most malignant elements in the father-son relationship is proximity without communication. It is extremely difficult for a boy to establish an appropriate identity, a sense of his individuality, with an unresponsive father.

I have observed that fathers who have shared in the childbirth experience talk about "*our* labor, *our* delivery." A family bonding takes place by virtue of the intensity of the emotional experience. "I feel quite actively involved with my children," said Seattle psychiatrist Nicholas Ward. "My wife and I went through childbirth preparation together. I was there, and what was remarkable was that I experienced everything that had been written about bonding: an instantaneous elation and love. All this intellectual stuff about competitive sons was out the window. I'm a psychiatrist and I look at things rationally, logically, in words, and most of what I experienced doesn't verbalize very well. I tried writing poetry about it. One image that came to mind was that he was hinged to my soul."

Fathers who experience the full range of childbirth preparation and delivery are much more involved with their children later on and more capable of expressing emotion. Richard Crim pointed out that "I participate very much in raising my son. I feel like it's where I belong, in a way. I don't feel my wife should do it alone. My feeling for my son had been growing through the nine months of Joan's pregnancy. So gradually an emotion grew in me. It was *amazing* when the baby was born. The euphoria I felt! Here was this ugly little creature wrapped in my arms, and he was a mess and it was getting all over my shirt, and I was trying to wrap him in a blanket and I felt so awkward. It was an instant I'd been prepared for, but when the baby came, the feeling was so much stronger. I cried. I let tears out and didn't feel ashamed about them at all."

Only recently have studies been conducted to determine the importance of the early father-infant relationship and the impact of the father on the development of the infant. This neglect, according to one report, stems, in part, from our assumption concerning the primacy of the mother-infant relationship, and secondly, from the belief that paternal influence assumes importance only in late infancy and early childhood. But evidence strongly suggests that fathers play an exceedingly influential role in the cognitive and social development of their children beginning in the *early postpartum stage.*

I believe the acceptance of males in the nurturant role is not only functional but will contribute to the survival of the family as a social unit. I would predict that there will be continued societal changes that will enable men to participate more fully in the lives of their children—paternity leaves, four-day workweeks, shorter workdays, househusbandry as common practice—to make it possible for both parents to fulfill what is surely the most important commitment of their lives.